Biergarten Cookbook

Forellen

Lachsforellen
(rotfleischige Forelle)

Makrelen

Saiblinge

Renken

Julia Skowronek

Biergarten Cookbook
Traditional Bavarian Recipes

Photography by Brigitte Sporrer

Contents

From pretzels, to cheese spreads, to sausage salads—delicious food to take along with you to a biergarten, or on a picnic. Each dish tastes especially good under chestnut trees and blue Bavarian skies dotted with fluffy white clouds.

From beer goulash, to cheese spaetzle, to steak with fried onions—classic biergarten dishes to make at home.

Apple fritters, juicy plum tart, and more—wonderful desserts to pack in a picnic basket. Pure summer happiness!

Biergartens and the Bavarian lifestyle

The "Mass" (liter) of beer gleams golden-yellow in the sun. Heavenly aromas of "Steckerlfisch" (grilled mackerel on a stick) and roast pork hocks waft through the air. At the next table, under the shade of chestnut trees, a man unpacks his "Brotzeit," a typical Bavarian snack or meal consisting of bread and something to go with it, such as cheese and sausage. This is a true Bavarian biergarten idyll and perfect summer happiness.

Everyone envies the Bavarians for their biergartens. After all, authentic biergarten culture is only found in the Free State of Bavaria. The custom of bringing one's own food to biergartens owes its origin to Maximilian I of Bavaria. In January 1812, he proclaimed that in June, July, August, and September, beer brewers would be allowed to serve beer brewed and stored in their own cellars, as well as bread, but not any other kinds of food and drink.

This was a diplomatic tour de force by the Bavarian King in response to angry protests of pub and restaurant owners. According to Bavarian biergarten rules dating back to 1539, beer brewing was only allowed during the cooler months of the year, between September 29 and April 23. In summer, the danger of fires from the hot beer brewing kettles was simply too high. Consequently, only flat, warm beer was available during the summer months, when thirst for beer was highest.

Munich's brewers found a solution. They built cellars and filled them with blocks of ice cut in winter. They also planted chestnut trees, whose thick foliage provided perfect shade for the beer. And, as a pleasant side effect, they were nice to sit under. A few chairs and tables, a cold beer from the cellar, a hearty snack to go with the beer, and the biergarten was invented.

People flocked to the biergartens in droves to drink, eat, and relax. Pub and restaurant owners were not pleased—their customers were being stolen away by the wildly proliferating biergartens. They complained, and succeeded in having the sale of beer banned in biergartens. An escalation of hostilities was inevitable until the King provided the solution with his decree: Beer sales would be allowed in biergartens, but patrons would have to bring their own cheese and sausage. Biergarten operators were not allowed to serve hot food in biergartens.

The biergarten revolt

Over the centuries, countless biergartens have been established. Large and small, they are found in the city and in the countryside, beside rivers, between houses, beside fields, and in front of Alpine panoramas. And the sale of hot food has been permitted for a long time now. The biergarten world remained intact until 1995, when residents living beside one of Munich's largest biergartens, Waldwirtschaft Großhesselohe, filed an official complaint. They objected that the biergarten was too loud. The court handed down its decision. In the future, the biergarten would have to close at 9:30pm.

A popular uproar ensued, leading to the first ever Bavarian biergarten revolt in the center of Munich and a petition protesting the end of traditional biergarten culture. The upshot was a new law, passed on April 20, 1999, and still valid today, regulating Bavarian biergartens. This law declares that biergartens, because of long-standing tradition, are a core part of Bavarian cultural heritage. It also declares that a biergarten is only then officially a biergarten when it has the character of a garden and allows patrons to consume, for free, food they have brought along. These characteristics distinguish biergartens from other outdoor restaurants. Another part of the ruling stipulates that biergartens must close by 11pm. Noteworthy is also the passage asserting that biergartens perform an important social and communicative function, stressing that biergartens have long been beloved meeting places for a wide spectrum of the populace. They enable people to come together informally, without constraint, in a way that helps overcome social differences. The conviviality of biergartens, and the chance of being together with others in the outdoors, helps counter feelings of loneliness.

Everyone is equal in a biergarten

In 2012, the biergarten celebrated its 200-year anniversary. Biergartens are as popular as ever. They are beloved by young and old, locals and tourists, eccentrics and groups of friends, punks, nerds, hipsters, managers, families, lovers, small children, dogs. The person at the next table might be a retiree or a student, a lawyer or a mail carrier. Elitism has no place in Bavarian biergartens.

It's up to you to find your own favorite biergarten. In Munich alone, there are over 100 of them to try. How can one decide? Perhaps it is the type of beer served, the size of the playground, the best spare ribs, the crispest pretzels, or the brass band. Some people have high expectations when it comes to the food they want. Others love really rustic food, or bring along their own—perhaps a sausage salad, or several kinds of cheese, white and red radishes, or a sweet treat. Or they might bring a homemade cheese spread, or hamburger patties with potato salad. There are recipes in this book for all these delicious dishes, and more.

Strangers' eyes always widen in surprise when not only food, but tablecloths, cutlery, napkins, and tea lights are dug out of the recesses of picnic baskets. They are just as surprised when entire children's birthday parties, including cake and party hats, or "Stammtische," regular gatherings of friends, move outdoors into the biergarten. All of this and more is permitted, as long as you buy your drinks from the counter! Because, fortunately, King Max said so in 1812. Prosit!

Cold snacks, salads, and more

Chilled cucumber soup with smoked trout

SERVES 4

Preparation time:
  20 minutes

1½ cucumbers
1 bunch of fresh dill
2 tbsp horseradish
  (from the jar)
freshly squeezed juice of
  1 lemon
1 cup buttermilk
5½oz (150g) crème fraîche
salt and pepper
1 tsp sugar
2 smoked trout fillets

1. Chop the cucumber into large pieces. Purée the cucumber, dill, horseradish, lemon juice, buttermilk, and crème fraîche in the blender. Season the soup with salt, pepper, and sugar and put it into the refrigerator to chill until serving time.

2. Cut up the trout fillets into bite-size pieces. Ladle the chilled soup into soup bowls and add the pieces of smoked trout.

TIP: The chilled cucumber soup tastes delicious on its own. You also can substitute thinly sliced strips of smoked salmon for the trout.

Chilled radish soup with fresh goat cheese

SERVES 4

Preparation time:
  20 minutes

1 bunch of radishes
1 ripe avocado
2 handfuls of spinach
  leaves
juice of 1 lemon
1 cup cold water
salt and pepper
1 tsp sugar
3½oz (100g) goat cheese

1. Wash and clean the radishes, reserving the radish greens. Slice the avocado in half lengthwise, remove the stone, and scoop out the avocado flesh.

2. Purée the avocado, radish greens, spinach, lemon juice, and water until smooth. Season the soup with salt, pepper, and sugar and place it into the refrigerator to chill until serving time.

3. Coarsely chop the radishes. Ladle the chilled soup into soup bowls and add the radish pieces. Crumble the fresh goat cheese and sprinkle it over the soup.

Obatzda—Bavarian cheese spread

This tasty spread made with ripe cheese is a biergarten classic, and really easy to prepare. If you like, you can stir in some beer!

1. In a bowl, break up the Brie or Camembert cheese into small pieces with a fork. Add the fresh cheese and mix everything together. Chop the chives finely and add them to the bowl. Season the spread with salt, pepper, and paprika, and stir.

2. Peel the onion and slice it into rings. Portion out the spread and decorate each portion with the onion rings. Serve with salt pretzels.

VARIATIONS: To make HERB OBATZDA, stir 1 handful of chopped mixed herbs (such as a mix of parsley, chervil, and basil) and 1 handful of chopped chives into the spread. Season to taste with salt and pepper.

TIP: Use Camembert cheese if you like a stronger cheese taste, Brie cheese if you like a milder cheese taste.

SERVES 4
Preparation time:
    20 minutes

7oz (200g) Brie cheese
    or Camembert cheese
7oz (200g) fresh cheese,
    such as ricotta cheese
    or mascarpone
1 bunch of chives
salt and pepper
1 tbsp sweet paprika
1 red onion
salt pretzels or sesame
    pretzels, for serving

Pear obatzda

This cheese spread surprises with its fruity flavor. It tastes especially good when it is made with local pears and walnuts.

SERVES 4

Preparation time:
   25 minutes

2 tbsp shelled walnuts
1 pear
1 tsp brown sugar
5½oz (150g) blue-veined
   cheese, such as
   Gorgonzola cheese
3½oz (100g) fresh cheese,
   such as ricotta cheese,
   cottage cheese, or cream
   cheese
salt and pepper
shelled walnuts and pear
   chips, for serving

1. Coarsely chop the walnuts. Fry them in a frying pan, without using any oil, stirring constantly until they are golden-brown in color. Remove from the frying pan and let cool.

2. Peel, quarter, and core the pear. Cut it into small cubes. Place the pear in a frying pan, sprinkle sugar over the top, and sauté for about 5 minutes until the pear is light-brown and the sugar is caramelized. Remove the pear from the frying pan and let cool.

3. In a bowl, break up the blue-veined cheese into small pieces with a fork. Add the fresh cheese and mix together. Stir in the walnuts and pears. Season to taste with salt and pepper.

4. Divide the cheese spread into portions and sprinkle walnuts over the top. Serve with pear chips on the side. Beer bread crescent rolls (see p. 56) go very well with this spread.

TIP: To make PEAR CHIPS, preheat the oven to 210°F (100°C). Thinly slice firm pears vertically. Cut out the cores. Line a baking tray with parchment paper. Arrange the slices in a single layer on the tray. Dry the slices of pear in the middle of the oven for about 2 hours. Store them in an airtight container.

Ham schmalz

1. Cut up the ham into small cubes. Place the ham and the lard in a small pot and simmer over low heat for about 20 minutes.

2. Pluck the thyme leaves from the sprigs and sprinkle them into the schmalz. Season the schmalz with salt and pepper and remove it from the stove. Leave it to cool. When it is cool, put it into the refrigerator for about 2 hours to harden.

SERVES 4
Preparation time:
  25 minutes
Refrigeration time:
  2 hours

1 thick slice hot-smoked
  ham (9oz/250g)
9oz (250g) pork lard
4 sprigs of thyme
salt and pepper

Apple and onion schmalz

1. Peel the onion and slice it into rings. Coarsely grate the unpeeled apple. Dredge the onion rings in the flour, then put them into a sieve and shake off the extra flour.

2. Heat the oil in a small pot. In small batches, fry the onion rings in the oil for about 3 minutes until they are crispy. Drain the rings on paper towels.

3. Over low heat, melt the vegetable shortening and oil in a small pot. Add the grated apple and cook it for about 5 minutes in the fat.

4. Stir the marjoram and the fried onions into the melted shortening. Season with salt and pepper, remove from the stove, and let cool. Then, put it into the refrigerator for about 2 hours to harden.

TIP: Ham schmalz and the vegetarian apple and onion schmalz taste very good as spreads on bread, such as beer bread (see p. 56). They also enhance the flavor of sauerkraut and pan-fried potatoes.

SERVES 4
Preparation time:
  25 minutes
Refrigeration time: 2 hours

1 onion
1 apple
3 tbsp all-purpose flour
oil, for frying
7oz (200g) vegetable
  shortening, such as
  palm oil, or coconut oil
  shortening
5 tbsp vegetable oil
½ tsp dried marjoram
salt and pepper

Top ten biergarten dishes

There is no limit to the imagination when it comes to conjuring up new dishes to bring along on the next biergarten outing. If you prefer the classic biergarten style, here are the absolute biergarten favorites, both hot and cold. And all those non-natives who live in Bavaria or are visiting for a while will definitely win points with their native Bavarian friends if they have these dishes in their repertoire.

Radish flowers with quark dip

Radishes look especially attractive on the table when they have been cut into roses. With a bit of practice, they are quick and easy to make.

SERVES 4

Preparation time:
  40 minutes

2 bunches of radishes
1 seedless cucumber
1 bunch of scallions
1lb 2oz (500g) quark
  (alternatively, use a
  thick and creamy, plain,
  non-fat yogurt)
7oz (200g) fresh cheese,
  such as ricotta cheese
  or mascarpone
freshly squeezed juice
  of ½ a lemon
salt and pepper

1. Remove the radish greens, leaving a bit of the stem on each radish. Reserve the greens.

2. Next, using a paring knife, cut the radishes into roses. To make radish roses, first cut out three small slices from the root end of each radish. Then, toward the top of the radish, cut horizontally into the radishes all the way around to create the petals. Place the radishes in a bowl of ice water to make the roses open up. Reserve the radish parings.

3. Cut the cucumber into small cubes. Cut the scallions into rings. Coarsely chop the radish greens.

4. Mix together the quark, fresh cheese, and lemon juice in a bowl. Stir in the radish parings, cucumber, scallions, and radish greens. Season with salt and pepper.

5. Remove the opened radish flowers from the ice water and serve them with the dip.

TIP: If you're in a hurry, this dip tastes just as good with plain radishes. You can also serve the dip with peppers, carrots, kohlrabi, and cucumbers, which adds even more color and flavor to the table.

Chickpea spread
with capers

1. Place the chickpeas in a sieve, rinse them with cold water, and drain. Chop the capers coarsely.

2. Purée the chickpeas, soy sauce, lemon juice, and oil. Stir in the yogurt and capers, and season the mixture with salt, pepper, and paprika. Serve the chickpea spread with fresh white bread or vegetable sticks for dipping.

SERVES 4
Preparation time:
   20 minutes

1 can of chickpeas
   (400g)
1 tbsp capers (from the jar)
1 dash soy sauce
freshly squeezed juice of
   ½ a lemon
2 tbsp cold-pressed
   sunflower oil
5½oz (150g) plain yogurt
salt and pepper
½ tsp paprika

Potato and
sour cream spread

1. Boil the potatoes in salted water for about 20 minutes or until they are done. Drain the potatoes, let the steam evaporate, and peel them. Then, mash them with a potato masher.

2. Peel the onion and chop it finely. Chop the parsley finely. Melt the butter in a small frying pan and sauté the onion.

3. Mix together the onion, parsley, sour cream, and potatoes. Season the mixture with salt and pepper, and serve either warm or cold as a spread. This spread makes a tasty small first course when it is served with daikon radish or radishes.

SERVES 4
Preparation time:
   25 minutes

14oz (400g) white potatoes,
   such as Russet potatoes
salt
1 onion
1 bunch of flat-leaf parsley
1 tbsp butter
7oz (200g) sour cream
pepper

Pepper sesame spread

This spread evokes delicious Asian flavors in the biergarten. Although it takes longer to prepare than many spreads, the work is worth it! Serve it with bread or with vegetable sticks for dipping.

SERVES 4

Preparation time:
   25 minutes
Soaking time: 4 hours
Roasting time: 25 minutes

4 tbsp sunflower seeds
1lb 2oz (500g) red bell
   peppers
1 tbsp black sesame seeds
2 tbsp brewer's yeast flakes
3 tbsp cold-pressed
   sunflower oil
salt and pepper

1. Place the sunflower seeds in a bowl, cover them with cold water, and let them soak for at least 4 hours. Drain the sunflower seeds and purée them.

2. Preheat the oven to 400°F (200°C). Line a baking tray with parchment paper. Wash the peppers and arrange them on the baking tray. Roast them in the middle of the oven for about 25 minutes, turning once, until the skin has started to blacken and blister. Remove the peppers from the oven, cover them with a wet, clean kitchen towel, and let cool.

3. In a frying pan, roast the black sesame seeds for about 5 minutes or until they begin to crackle. Remove the frying pan from the heat and let cool.

4. Using a sharp knife, remove the skin from the peppers. Slice them in half lengthwise. Remove the stems, ribs, and seeds. Dice the peppers finely.

5. In a bowl, mix together the puréed sunflower seeds, diced peppers, sesame seeds, brewer's yeast flakes, and sunflower oil. Season to taste with salt and pepper.

VARIATION: To make PAPRIKA FETA CHEESE DIP, omit the brewer's yeast and the sunflower oil. Instead, stir in 5½oz (150g) of finely crumbled Feta cheese.

Sweet mustard

1. Heat up a frying pan. Roast the mustard seeds for about 5 minutes or until they crackle. Crush the mustard seeds in a mortar until medium-coarse. Place them in a bowl, add the mustard powder and sugar, and stir.

2. Place the vinegar, 7fl oz (200ml) water, cloves, coriander, and lemon peel in a small pot. Bring everything to a boil and reduce the liquid to about 5 tablespoons.

3. Pour the liquid through a fine-meshed sieve into the bowl containing the mustard seeds. Add the honey and stir everything together. If needed, thin with water.

4. Pour the mustard into the jar and close it. Let the flavor develop for 4 to 6 weeks in the refrigerator, as desired. Serve with mild sausages or add to a salad dressing.

MAKES 7FL OZ (200 ML)
Preparation time:
  20 minutes
Refrigeration time:
  4–6 weeks

4 tbsp whole mustard seeds
1 tbsp mustard powder
2 tbsp brown sugar
4 tbsp sherry vinegar
2 cloves
½ tsp coriander seeds
peel from an organic lemon
  (about 1in/3cm long)
2 tbsp honey

YOU WILL ALSO NEED
1 medium jam jar

Hot tarragon mustard

1. Combine the mustard powder, sugar, and salt in a bowl. Place the vinegar, 7fl oz (200ml) of water, cloves, coriander, and 1 tarragon sprig into a small pot. Bring to a boil and reduce to about 5 tablespoons.

2. Set a fine-meshed sieve over the bowl containing the mustard powder. Pour the liquid through the sieve and stir. Finely chop the second tarragon sprig and add it to the mustard. If needed, thin the mustard with a bit of water. Pour the mustard into the jar and close it. Let the mustard flavor develop for 4 to 6 weeks in the refrigerator, as desired.

3. Tarragon mustard goes really well with hot dogs, pork sausages (see p. 95), and hamburger patties (see p. 91).

MAKES 7FL OZ (200 ML)
Preparation time:
  20 minutes
Refrigeration time:
  4–6 weeks

4 tbsp yellow mustard
  powder
4 tbsp sugar
salt
4 tbsp sherry vinegar
2 cloves
½ tsp coriander seeds
2 sprigs of tarragon

YOU WILL ALSO NEED
1 medium jam jar

Savory butter spreads

These compound butters are quickly prepared and taste heavenly on freshly baked bread. They freeze well, too, making them ideal for those last-minute biergarten excursions.

SERVES 8
Preparation time: 1 hour

FOR THE HERB BUTTER
9oz (250g) unsalted butter
salt and pepper
1 handful of freshly
   chopped mixed herbs
   (such as parsley,
   chives, dill)
1 squeeze of lemon juice
½ tsp chili flakes

FOR THE TOMATO BUTTER
9oz (250g) unsalted butter
salt and pepper
5 sun-dried tomatoes
1 handful of small-leaf basil
2 tbsp tomato paste

**FOR THE LEMON PEPPER
BUTTER**
9oz (250g) unsalted butter
salt and pepper
1 tbsp mixed peppercorns
zest of ½ an organic lemon
freshly squeezed juice of
   ½ a lemon

FOR THE GARLIC BUTTER
1 head of garlic
9oz (250g) unsalted butter
salt and pepper

1. To make the herb butter, soften the butter and cream it in a bowl. Season to taste with salt and pepper. Stir in the herbs, lemon juice, and chili flakes.

2. To make the tomato butter, soften the butter and cream it in a bowl. Season to taste with salt and pepper. Finely chop the sun-dried tomatoes and stir them into the butter along with the basil leaves and tomato paste.

3. To make the lemon pepper butter, soften the butter and cream it in a bowl. Season to taste with salt and pepper. Coarsely crush the peppercorns in a mortar. Stir the pepper, lemon zest, and lemon juice into the butter.

4. To make the garlic butter, preheat the oven to 350°F (180°C). Place the head of garlic, unpeeled, on the oven rack and roast in the middle of the oven for 25 minutes. Break up the head of garlic into cloves, squeeze the roasted garlic out of the peel, and chop finely. Soften the butter and cream it in a bowl. Season to taste with salt and pepper and stir in the garlic.

TIP: Keep the butter spreads in the refrigerator until serving time. The spreads are best filled into small jam jars so you can easily take them with you to the biergarten, or on a picnic. To freeze the spreads, divide them into portions, and wrap them in plastic wrap. Remove the portions from the freezer as needed.

Bavarian sausage salad

Sausage salad is an undisputed biergarten favorite. Its tart marinade means that it goes really well with a freshly poured beer, especially on hot summer days.

1. Remove the sausage casings. Thinly slice the sausage and the dill pickles, and place them in a bowl.

2. Add the vinegar, dill pickle liquid, and oil to the bowl, season with salt and pepper, and toss gently. Leave the sausage salad to marinate for about 15 minutes.

3. Peel the onions and cut them into rings. Chop the chives. Portion out the sausage salad and scatter the onion and chopped chives over the top. Serve with bread, soft pretzels, or pan-fried potatoes.

TIP: BAVARIAN SAUSAGE SALAD is traditionally made with Regensburg sausages, which are smoked, stubby, boiled sausages prepared with pork. It also tastes very good when made with other kinds of deli sausages such as beerwurst, turkey or ham kielbasa, mortadella, or bologna.

SERVES 4
Preparation time:
   10 minutes
Marinating time:
   15 minutes

1⅓lb (600g) cooked deli
   sausage, such as
   Regensburg, bologna,
   beerwurst, or kielbasa
   sausage
4 dill pickles
   (from the jar)
4 tbsp sherry vinegar
4 tbsp dill pickle liquid
   (from the jar)
4 tbsp vegetable oil
salt and pepper
2 red onions
1 bunch of chives

Swiss sausage salad

This colorful sausage salad tastes delicious both in the biergarten and at home. For a simple variation, use onions thinly sliced into rings instead of the cucumber, scallions, and tomatoes.

SERVES 4

Preparation time:
  10 minutes
Marinating time:
  15 minutes

14oz (400g) thinly sliced cooked deli sausage such as bologna, mortadella, or kielbasa sausage
7oz (200g) Emmenthal cheese
½ seedless cucumber
1 bunch of scallions
9oz (250g) cherry tomatoes
4 tbsp white wine vinegar
4 tbsp vegetable oil
salt and pepper

1. Slice the cooked sausage and Emmenthal cheese into thin strips and place them in a bowl.

2. Cut the half cucumber in two lengthwise and cut into slices. Cut the scallions into rings. Cut the tomatoes in half. Add the cucumber, scallions, and tomatoes to the sausage and cheese, and toss.

3. Add the vinegar and oil to the salad. Season with salt and pepper and toss well. Let the salad marinate for about 15 minutes. Serve with bread, soft pretzels, or pan-fried potatoes.

TIP: In Bavaria, this salad is often made with "Leberkaese," a typical Bavarian baked luncheon meat. But it tastes just as delicious made with other kinds of cooked sausage. You can also vary the cheese. Instead of Emmenthal cheese, try Gouda cheese, Tilsiter cheese, or Camembert cheese. And, if you like a bit of a crunch in your salad, add sliced red radishes, daikon radish, or red bell peppers.

Boiled beef salad with pumpkin seed oil

1. To cook the beef, fill a large pot with 6 cups of salted water and bring it to a boil. Place the meat in the water and let it cook at a rolling boil for about 5 minutes. Reduce the heat, skim off anything that rises to the surface, and gently simmer the beef for about 2 hours until it is tender. Ensure that the beef is always just barely covered with broth. Add more water as needed.

2. Cut the celery and carrots into large pieces. Cut the leek into slices. About 30 minutes before the beef is cooked, add the celery, carrots, leek, parsley, bay leaf, clove, juniper berries, and peppercorns to the pot.

3. Remove the beef from the pot and let it cool. Pour the broth into a bowl through a sieve lined with cheesecloth. Reserve the broth for a soup or for a hot boiled-beef dish.

4. To make the salad, slice the carrots and zucchini into thin strips. Blanch the carrots and zucchini in boiling salted water until tender but still firm to the bite. Plunge them into ice water. Slice the scallions into rings.

5. Carve the beef into very thin slices. Arrange the slices on four plates and scatter the blanched vegetables and scallions over top. Combine the salt, pepper, vinegar, and oil to make a dressing. Pour the dressing over the plates and let the salad marinate for 15 minutes. Just before serving, drizzle with pumpkin seed oil.

TIP: This is also delicious served hot. Carve the beef into inch-thick slices, ladle out a bit of broth over the beef, and garnish with chopped chives. Serve with parslied potatoes and fresh horseradish.

SERVES 4
Preparation time:
  40 minutes
Cooking time: 2 hours
Marinating time:
  15 minutes

FOR THE BOILED BEEF
salt
2.2lb (1kg) beef
  (chuck or shoulder)
2oz (60g) celery root
2oz (60g) carrots
3oz (90g) leek
4 sprigs of parsley
1 bay leaf
1 clove
1 tsp juniper berries
1 tsp black peppercorns

FOR THE SALAD
2 medium carrots
1 medium zucchini
salt
1 bunch of scallions
pepper
4 tbsp red wine vinegar
2 tbsp vegetable oil
4 tbsp pumpkin seed oil

Tangy cheese salad

SERVES 4
Preparation time:
    20 minutes

14oz (400g) pungent cheese
    such as Muenster cheese,
    Limburger cheese, or
    Romadur cheese
salt and pepper
4 tbsp sherry vinegar
4 tbsp vegetable oil
2 onions
1 tbsp paprika
1 tsp caraway seeds

1. Slice the cheese and portion it out onto four plates. Make a salad dressing by mixing together the salt, pepper, vinegar, and oil. Pour the dressing over the cheese and leave to marinate.

2. Peel the onions and cut them into rings. Sprinkle the paprika onto a small plate and dip the onion rings in the paprika.

3. Distribute the sliced onion over the cheese. Sprinkle the cheese with caraway seeds and serve.

TIP: A pungent, aromatic cheese such as Limburger is needed to make this salad stand out. But, since the cheese has a penetrating smell, make sure you don't leave it out for too long when serving it inside.

Cheese and pepper salad

SERVES 4
Preparation time:
    25 minutes

14oz (400g) Emmenthal
1 onion
1 red bell pepper
1 yellow bell pepper
1 green bell pepper
salt and pepper
1 tsp paprika
1 tsp smoked paprika
4 tbsp white wine vinegar
4 tbsp vegetable oil

1. Slice the Emmenthal cheese thinly and place the strips in a bowl. Peel the onion and slice it into rings. Slice the peppers into fine strips. Mix together the cheese, onion rings, and strips of pepper.

2. Sprinkle the salt, pepper, and paprika over the salad. Add the vinegar and oil, toss well, and let the salad marinate for about 15 minutes.

TIP: Adding smoked paprika gives the CHEESE AND PEPPER SALAD a tantalizing light, smoky flavor.

Bread dumpling salad

1. To make the bread dumplings, cut the bread rolls into thin slices and place them in a bowl. Boil the milk and pour it over the bread. Mix the bread and milk together. Let stand for about 15 minutes.

2. Peel and dice the onion. Melt the butter in a small frying pan, add the onion, and sauté until tender. Add the onion to the bread. Chop the parsley finely. Add the parsley and eggs to the bread and combine well. Season with salt, pepper, and nutmeg.

3. In a large pot, bring salted water to a boil. Using your hands, shape peach-sized dumplings from the dough. Place the dumplings in the boiling water and return the water to a boil. Reduce the heat and gently poach the dumplings for about 20 minutes. Using a slotted spoon, remove the dumplings from the pot and let cool.

4. To make the salad, peel and chop the onions. Wash the radishes and cut them into fine strips.

5. Slice the dumplings and place them in a bowl. Make a dressing from the salt, pepper, vinegar, and oil. Drizzle the dressing over the dumplings and gently toss everything together. Let the salad steep for about 15 minutes.

6. Sprinkle the onions and radishes over the salad. Wash the shoots, pat them dry, and scatter them over the salad.

TIP: Before cooking the entire batch, make a test dumpling. Shape one dumpling and boil as described above. If the dumpling falls apart in the water, add some bread crumbs to the mixture. If it is too firm, add another egg. Test again.

SERVES 4
Preparation time: 1 hour
Soaking time: 15 minutes
Marinating time:
    15 minutes

FOR THE BREAD DUMPLINGS
8 day-old bread rolls
1 cup whole milk
1 onion
1 tbsp butter
1 bunch of flat-leaf parsley
2 large eggs
salt and pepper
1 pinch of ground nutmeg

FOR THE SALAD
2 white or red onions
½ bunch of radishes
salt and pepper
4 tbsp sherry vinegar
4 tbsp vegetable oil
2 tbsp shoots, such as pea
    shoots or watercress
    shoots

Bavarian potato salad

Bavarian potato salad with vinegar-and-oil dressing goes extremely well with many biergarten dishes. And, because it is so wonderfully variable, there are many ways to build on the basic recipe.

SERVES 4
Preparation time:
35 minutes
Marinating time:
15 minutes

1¾lb (750g) yellow potatoes, such as Yukon Gold
salt and pepper
1 onion
4 tbsp vegetable oil
3 tbsp white wine vinegar
1 cup vegetable broth
1 tbsp mustard

1. Boil the potatoes, unpeeled, in salted water for about 20 minutes or until they are done. Drain, allow some of the steam to evaporate, and peel. Let the potatoes cool a bit, cut them into slices, and place them in a bowl.

2. Peel the onion and chop it finely. Heat the oil in a frying pan and sauté the onion. Add the vinegar and vegetable broth, stir in the mustard, and bring to a boil.

3. Pour the hot marinade over the potatoes and toss. Season the potato salad with salt and pepper. Serve with hamburger patties (see p. 91) or schnitzel (see p. 80).

TIP: Bavarian potato salad, in all its various forms, tastes better if it is allowed to sit for at least 15 minutes before it is served.

VARIATIONS: To make POTATO AND CUCUMBER SALAD, cut 1 seedless cucumber in half lengthwise, slice the halves thinly, add them to the salad, and toss. To make POTATO SALAD WITH ARUGULA AND BACON, cut a piece of smoked, well-marbled bacon weighing 5½oz (150g) into small cubes. Fry the bacon in 1 tablespoon of vegetable oil until crisp. Add the bacon and 2 bunches of arugula to the salad and toss. To make POTATO SALAD WITH MÂCHE AND PUMPKIN SEED OIL, add 2 handfuls of mâche to the salad and toss, then drizzle 4 tablespoons of pumpkin seed oil over top. To make POTATO SALAD WITH RADISHES AND SCALLIONS, cut the radish greens off 1 bunch of radishes and chop coarsely. Slice the radishes and 1 bunch of scallions. Add to the salad and toss.

Pasta salad with tomatoes and mozzarella

Many locals call Munich the most northerly of all Italian cities. This is why Italian pasta salad, with its southern flair, is right at home in the biergarten. It is also very easy to take along.

1. Cook the pasta in boiling salted water, following the directions on the package, until the pasta is cooked but still firm to the bite. Pour the pasta into a colander, rinse it with cold water, and let drain. Place the pasta in a bowl.

2. Place the cherry tomatoes in a large freezer bag. Seal the bag tightly and crush the tomatoes in the bag. Add the tomatoes along with their juices to the pasta.

3. Season the pasta with salt, pepper, and Sambal Oelek. Drizzle olive oil over the top, toss, and let sit for about 15 minutes.

4. To serve, add the spinach leaves and mozzarella balls to the salad and toss. This cold pasta dish is excellent either as a main dish or as a side dish, for example for hamburger patties (see p. 91) or roast chicken (see p. 76).

TIP: The ingredients can be altered easily. The salad also tastes very good made with Feta cheese or grilled halloumi cheese instead of mozzarella cheese, and made with arugula or mixed herb salad leaves instead of spinach. You can also, if you like, mix in some sliced bell pepper, cucumber, or fried cubes of zucchini and eggplant.

SERVES 4

Preparation time:
    25 minutes
Marinating time:
    15 minutes

9oz (250g) short pasta, such as penne, rotini, or farfalle
salt
9oz (250g) red cherry tomatoes
9oz (250g) yellow cherry tomatoes
pepper
1 tbsp Sambal Oelek
4 tbsp olive oil
2 handfuls of baby spinach leaves
10½oz (300g) mozzarella balls

Fried chicken with mixed salad

This is a real biergarten classic, one that can be enjoyed with a colorful, summery, tossed salad and with no feelings of guilt afterward.

SERVES 4
Preparation time:
  50 minutes

FOR THE FRIED CHICKEN
salt
1 roasting chicken, cut
  into eight pieces
  (about 2½lb / 1.2kg)
pepper
2 large eggs
4–5 tbsp all-purpose flour
4–5 tbsp bread crumbs
2 tbsp sesame seeds
vegetable oil, for deep
  frying
1 lemon, quartered

FOR THE SALAD
½ seedless cucumber
1 bunch of radishes
2 red bell peppers or red
  Cubanelle peppers
1 handful of red cherry
  tomatoes
2 medium carrots
4 handfuls of mixed lettuce
  leaves
salt and pepper
3 tbsp vinegar
4 tbsp vegetable oil

1. To make the fried chicken, bring a large pot of salted water to a boil. Add the chicken, reduce the heat, and let the chicken simmer gently for about 10 minutes. Remove the chicken. Let it cool for 10 minutes. Then, remove the skin and season the pieces of chicken with salt and pepper.

2. Whisk the eggs in a soup plate. Place the flour and bread crumbs on separate plates. Add the sesame seeds to the bread crumbs and mix together.

3. Dip the chicken pieces into the flour. Shake off the excess flour. Dip the chicken into the beaten eggs and then dip it into the bread crumbs, firmly pressing down on the chicken to coat it well. Shake off the excess bread crumbs.

4. To make the salad, cut the cucumber in half lengthwise. Cut the cucumber halves and the radishes into slices. Cut the peppers into strips, halve the tomatoes, and grate the carrots. Add the lettuce leaves and toss.

5. Combine the salt, pepper, vinegar, and oil. Drizzle it over the salad, toss, and portion out the salad onto four plates.

6. Fill a deep pot about half-full of frying oil. Fry the chicken, a few pieces at a time, for about 5 minutes until it is brown and crisp. Remove the chicken pieces from the frying oil and drain them on paper towels. Arrange the chicken on top of the salad. Serve with the wedges of lemon.

Red cabbage slaw with oranges

1. Shred the cabbage finely. Place it in a bowl. Salt liberally. Using your hands, vigorously knead the cabbage for about 5 minutes or until the cabbage has softened.

2. Roast the sunflower seeds in a frying pan, stirring constantly until they are golden-brown. Let cool.

3. Grate the carrots. Peel the oranges and cut out the segments. Reserve the orange juice.

4. Stir the sunflower seeds, carrots, orange segments, orange juice, marmalade, vinegar, and oil into the cabbage. Season the salad with pepper and leave to marinate for about 15 minutes. Serve this slaw with roast duck (see p. 88) or spare ribs (see p. 83).

SERVES 4
Preparation time:
   30 minutes
Marinating time:
   15 minutes

1 small head of red cabbage
   (about 1¾lb/800g)
salt
2 tbsp sunflower seeds
2 medium carrots
2 oranges
1 tbsp orange marmalade
2 tbsp red wine vinegar
4 tbsp vegetable oil
pepper

Slaw with bacon

1. Cut the cabbage into very fine strips and place it in a bowl. Salt generously. Using your hands, vigorously knead the cabbage for about 5 minutes until the cabbage has softened and released its juices.

2. Cut the bacon into small cubes. Heat the oil in a frying pan, add the bacon, and fry it until it is crisp. Add the bacon, frying oil, and vinegar to the cabbage. Toss well.

3. Season the salad to taste with pepper, add the caraway seeds, and let it marinate for about 15 minutes. This slaw goes very well with roast pork (see p. 79) or spare ribs (see p. 83).

SERVES 4
Preparation time:
   20 minutes
Marinating time:
   15 minutes

1 small head of white
   cabbage (about
   1¾lb/800g)
salt
5½oz (150g) smoked bacon
4 tbsp vegetable oil
4 tbsp white wine vinegar
   pepper
1 tsp caraway seeds

Green bean salad with Feta cheese

A simple green bean salad is pepped up in this recipe with tomatoes and Feta cheese. It is a fine combination, one that tastes just as good on its own as it does when served with grilled or pan-fried meat.

SERVES 4
Preparation time:
  40 minutes

1¾lb (800g) green beans
salt
4 tomatoes
freshly squeezed juice
  of 1 lemon
4 tbsp olive oil
pepper
7oz (200g) Feta cheese

1. Trim the beans. Bring a large pot of salted water to a rolling boil. Blanch the beans for about 5 minutes until they are tender but firm to the bite. Then, plunge the beans into a bowl of ice water and let drain in a sieve.

2. Dice the tomatoes and place them in a bowl. Add the beans. Pour in the lemon juice and olive oil, and season with salt and pepper. Toss the salad briefly and let it marinate for about 15 minutes.

3. Portion out the green bean salad onto four plates and crumble the Feta cheese over the top. Serve as a light main course with white bread or to accompany dishes such as spare ribs (see p. 83) or pork hocks (see p. 79).

Hops and malt forever: Bavarian beer and the purity law

Bavarian beer—pure pleasure

The beer lover shudders. Ox bile, juniper berries, sloe, oak bark, fir chips, pine roots, and all sorts of herbs in his or her favorite beer! A new scandal? No, no, don't worry, this happened a long time ago. In the 16th century, people had to put up with many kinds of adulterated beer. To put a stop to this, the reigning Bavarian Duke, Herzog Wilhelm IV, passed a law in April 1516 dealing with how beer in the land was to be served and brewed in summer and winter. The ruling stipulates that "... in the future, we command that in all our cities and markets, and in the entire countryside, no beer shall contain anything other than barley, hops, and water."

Thus was the "purity law" proclaimed, the oldest still-enforced law governing food production. This meant no artificial flavors, no chemical additives, and no sugar. Even today, the law is followed by each of the more than 600 Bavarian breweries. Together, they produce approximately 40 types and 4,000 brands of beer. Not only are there the large breweries, such as Paulaner, Spaten, Löwenbräu, and others, that distribute throughout Germany and export to other countries worldwide. There are also countless regional breweries with special types of beer much appreciated by beer connoisseurs. Even if you tried a different brand of beer each day, you would be kept busy for almost 11 years! What a great prospect for beer lovers in Bavaria.

Although beer is practically synonymous with Bavaria, Bavarians did not invent beer brewing. Almost 4,000 years ago, a Sumerian baker accidentally discovered a brew with an inebriating effect. The Egyptians and Romans knew how to make beer, too. In central Europe, monks started to brew beer about 1,000 years ago. They were highly professional, full of zeal—and they were brewers out of self-interest; during Lent, a time of fasting, the rule of thumb was "liquids do not break a fast." Beer kept the monks in a cheerful mood. The official anniversary of the art of brewing in Bavaria is 1040. This is when the City of Freising granted the Benedictine monastery brewery a license to brew and sell the beer they brewed. In 1372, a brewing charter allowed anyone to brew beer who was able to afford it. This hardly improved the quality of beer, but it did inspire creativity until the beer purity law was passed. After that, unadulterated pleasure was guaranteed.

Soft pretzels

No biergarten visit is complete without pretzels! There are many legends about their invention, but one thing is certain—everyone loves them. Making them yourself is easier than you think.

1. Sift the flour into a large mixing bowl. Make a well in the center. Crumble the yeast into the well. Add the sugar and some lukewarm water. Stirring in the well, incorporate some flour into the liquid. Cover the bowl with a kitchen towel. Leave in a warm place to rise for about 20 minutes.

2. Add the oil, salt, and 4 tablespoons of lukewarm water to the bowl. Using your fingers, mix everything together to make a dough. Using your hands, knead the dough vigorously. Let it rise in a warm place for about 1 hour.

3. Knead the dough again vigorously and divide into eight portions. Roll the portions into logs about 16" (40cm) long and 1in (3cm) thick. Shape them into pretzels. Cover the pretzels and let them rest for about 20 minutes.

4. Preheat the oven to 400°F (200°C). Line a baking tray with parchment paper. Dust it with flour. Place 4 cups of water in a pot, add the baking soda, and bring to a boil.

5. Using a slotted spoon, place the pretzels in the boiling soda solution, then let them boil for about 2 minutes, basting often. Remove them carefully, arrange them on the baking tray, and sprinkle them with coarse salt. Bake them in the middle of the oven for about 15 minutes.

TIP: Although the soda solution is edible, make sure it doesn't come into contact with aluminum to avoid unwanted chemical reactions.

MAKES 8 PRETZELS
Preparation time: 1 hour
Rising time: 95 minutes
Baking time: 15 minutes

1lb 2oz (500g) all-purpose flour, plus more for the work surface
¾oz (20g) cake yeast or 1 tsp active dry yeast
1 pinch of sugar
2 tbsp vegetable oil
salt
⅓ cup (40g) baking soda
coarse salt, for sprinkling

Beer bread with spices

MAKES 2 LOAVES
(12 SLICES EACH)
Preparation time:
    15 minutes
Rising time: 1 hour and
    30 minutes
Baking time: 1 hour

1 tsp coriander seeds
1 tsp caraway seeds
1 tsp anise seeds
1 tsp fennel seeds
14oz (400g) all-purpose
    flour, plus more for the
    work surface
1⅓lb (600g) dark rye flour
salt
1 tsp sugar
1 tbsp white vinegar
2 packages active dry yeast
4 tbsp sunflower seeds
2 cups beer
3 tbsp vegetable oil

1. In a mortar, coarsely crush the coriander, caraway, anise, and fennel seeds. Reserve 1 tablespoon for later use.

2. Place the spices, the flour, salt, sugar, vinegar, yeast, and sunflower seeds in a bowl. Pour in the beer, oil, and 7fl oz (200ml) of lukewarm water. Using your fingers, mix everything together to make a dough. Turn out the dough onto a floured work surface. Using your hands, knead vigorously. Cover with a kitchen towel and let rise for about 45 minutes.

3. Knead the dough again vigorously, divide it into two portions, and shape each portion into a loaf. Leave the loaves to rest for another 45 minutes.

4. Preheat the oven to 400°F (200°C). Line a baking tray with parchment paper. Dust it with flour. Place the loaves on the baking tray. Put a small bowl of water in the oven to bake along with the loaves. Brush the loaves with water and sprinkle with the remaining spices. Bake them in the middle of the oven for about 1 hour. Remove the loaves from the oven and let them cool.

VARIATION: To make BEER BREAD CRESCENT ROLLS (24 rolls), prepare the dough as described above and let it rise for 45 minutes. Then, on a floured work surface, roll out the dough the thickness of a finger. Using a dough wheel cutter, cut out 24 palm-sized triangles. Roll up the triangles, starting at the widest edge, and shape them into crescents. Place the rolls on a baking tray lined with parchment paper. Let them rise for 20 minutes. Brush the rolls with water and sprinkle with the rest of the spice mixture and coarse salt. Preheat the oven to 400°F (200°C). Place a small bowl of water in the oven. Bake the rolls in the middle of the oven for about 15 minutes.

Biergarten food for vegetarians

Hearty meat dishes are, without doubt, the stars of the Bavarian kitchen. But limited budgets and the Catholic meatless Friday in Bavaria ensured that numerous vegetarian dishes were also invented. Here is a selection of spreads, salads, and more that will delight vegetarians, too.

Roast pork in aspic

Aspics can be made in countless variations using cooked meat, fowl, fish, and vegetables. The aspic liquid itself can be flavored in many ways. And you can add, as desired, chopped herbs, marinated vegetables, hard-boiled eggs, and different vinegars.

1. Dissolve the gelatin powder in water, following the directions on the package. Add the vinegar.

2. Arrange the slices of cold roast pork on four shallow soup plates and pour about half of the aspic over the pork. Chill the plates in the refrigerator for about 30–60 minutes, until the first layer of aspic is slightly firm but not completely set.

3. In the meantime, cook the eggs for 8–10 minutes until they are hard-boiled. Rinse the eggs under cold water, peel them, and cut them into slices. Cut the dill pickles into slices, and cut the cherry tomatoes in half.

4. Arrange the sliced eggs, dill pickles, and tomatoes decoratively over the sliced pork. Cover with the remaining aspic and return the plates to the refrigerator. Chill the plates for at least 4 hours or, even better, overnight, until the aspic is completely set.

5. Just before serving, take the plates out of the refrigerator. Pan-fried potatoes (see p. 80) or a simple slice of buttered bread go very well with the pork aspics.

TIP: You can also prepare the aspic in a loaf pan. Line a loaf pan with plastic wrap, pour in a thin layer of aspic, layer the pork, eggs, pickles, and tomatoes, then pour in the remaining aspic. Refrigerate the aspic until it is completely set. Turn out the aspic and cut it into slices. You can also make the aspic using small molds or cups.

SERVES 4
Preparation time:
    15 minutes
Refrigeration time:
    5 hours

1oz (25g) unflavored
    powdered gelatin
3 tbsp sherry vinegar
4–8 slices cold roast pork
2 large eggs
2 dill pickles
1 handful of red cherry
    tomatoes

Radishes, open-faced chive sandwiches, and small hamburgers

Sliced daikon radish, red radishes, open-faced chive sandwiches, and bite-size patties are enormously popular in the biergarten. Just place everything on the table at once and the food will quickly disappear.

SERVES 4
Preparation time:
  45 minutes

1 hamburger patties recipe
  (see p. 91)
1 bunch of chives
4 slices of farmer's bread
butter, for the bread
1 daikon radish
1 bunch of radishes
salt

1. To make bite-size hamburger patties, prepare hamburger meat as described on page 91. Shape the hamburger meat into small patties and fry them.

2. To make the open-faced chive sandwiches, chop the chives finely and scatter them on a plate. Butter the slices of bread. Press the buttered side of the bread into the chives. Cut the slices in half or quarter them.

3. To make the plate of radish, slice the daikon radish as thinly as possible. Sprinkle the remaining chives over the radish.

4. Keeping the radishes together in the bunch, wash them thoroughly. Place the meat patties, open-faced chive sandwiches, daikon radish, and radishes on the table at the same time. Add salt to the radishes only once they are on the table. Serve with homemade tarragon mustard (see p. 29).

TIP: In Bavaria, you can buy spiral radish cutters in any store selling household wares. This little tool effortlessly turns daikon radishes and other types of fruit and vegetables into decorative spirals.

Cheese balls in oil

1. Dice the roasted peppers finely. Using your hands, shape balls the size of walnuts from the fresh cheese.

2. Pack alternating layers of diced pepper and fresh cheese balls in the jar. Add the rosemary, thyme, and peppercorns. Pour in enough oil to ensure that all the ingredients are completely covered. Seal the jar and leave to marinate in the refrigerator for at least 24 hours.

3. Serve the cheese balls as a spread for fresh crusty bread or with a salad.

MAKES 2 CUPS/500ML
Preparation time:
    15 minutes
Marinating time: 24 hours

2 roasted red peppers (from
    the jar)
7oz (200g) fresh cheese
    (ricotta cheese, cottage
    cheese, or cream cheese)
1 sprig of rosemary
1 sprig of thyme
½ tsp black peppercorns
cold pressed sunflower oil

YOU WILL ALSO NEED
1 large jam jar

Feta cheese in oil

1. Cut the lemon into slices. Cut the chili pepper into rings. Cut the feta cheese into chunks.

2. Pack alternating layers of the feta cheese, lemon, and green and black olives in the jar. Add the chili pepper and bay leaf. Pour in enough oil to ensure that all the ingredients are completely covered. Seal the jar and leave to marinate in the refrigerator for at least 24 hours.

3. Feta cheese in oil goes very well with salad, bread, or as a substitute for mozzarella in a pasta salad (see p. 45).

MAKES 2 CUPS/500ML
Preparation time:
    15 minutes
Marinating time: 24 hours

½ organic lemon
1 red chili pepper
7oz (200g) Feta cheese
2–3 tbsp green olives
2–3 tbsp black olives
1 bay leaf
olive oil

YOU WILL ALSO NEED
1 large jam jar

Pink pickled eggs

MAKES 1 LARGE MASON JAR
Preparation time:
   25 minutes
Cooking time: 45 minutes
Marinating time: 24 hours

2 small red beets
salt
10 eggs
5fl oz (150ml) red beet juice
2½fl oz (75ml) apple
   vinegar
1 tsp mustard seeds
½ tsp black peppercorns
2 cloves
1 bay leaf
1 tbsp sugar

1. Boil the whole beets in salted water for about 45 minutes. Drain and peel the beets and cut them into slices. Cook the eggs for 8–10 minutes until they are hard-boiled, rinse them in cold water, and peel.

2. Alternate layers of sliced beet and eggs in a large mason jar. In a pot, bring the red beet juice, vinegar, 1½ cups of water, mustard, peppercorns, cloves, bay leaf, and sugar to a boil. Pour the hot liquid over the eggs.

3. Seal the jar right away and leave the eggs to marinate in the refrigerator for at least 24 hours. To serve, cut the pickled eggs in half and sprinkle them with salt. Serve the slices of beet as a salad on the side. The pickled eggs will keep for up to 1 week in the refrigerator.

Pickled eggs

MAKES 1 LARGE MASON JAR
Preparation time:
   15 minutes
Marinating time: 3 days

10 large eggs
9oz (250g) shallots
¼ cup light balsamic
   vinegar
4 tbsp dark balsamic
   vinegar
2 sprigs of tarragon
½ tsp black peppercorns
½ tsp allspice berries
2 bay leaves
salt

1. Cook the eggs for 8–10 minutes until they are hard-boiled. Rinse them in cold water, crack the shells on all sides, and pack the eggs into a large mason jar.

2. Peel the shallots and slice them into rings. In a pot, bring the shallots, the two kinds of vinegar, 1½ cups of water, tarragon, pepper, allspice, bay leaves, and shallots to a boil. Pour the hot liquid over the eggs.

3. Seal the jar immediately and leave the eggs to marinate in the refrigerator for at least 3 days. To serve, cut the pickled eggs in half and sprinkle them with salt. The pickled eggs, perfect for every biergarten picnic, will keep for up to 1 week in the refrigerator.

Homemade dill pickles

Dill pickles add freshness and crunchiness to any biergarten buffet. They are quickly made. Packed in a pretty jar with a handmade label, they are a good gift to bring the next time you are invited to a biergarten feast and will certainly make a good impression.

1. Wash the pickling cucumbers thoroughly, place them in a bowl, and sprinkle with the salt. Cover them with water and put them into the refrigerator for 12 hours or overnight. Drain the cucumbers, rinse them with cold water, and place them on a clean kitchen towel to drain.

2. Peel the onion and slice it into rings. Cut the carrots and horseradish root into slices. Place equal amounts of the cucumbers, onion rings, carrots, horseradish, tarragon, dill, and pickling spice into each jar.

3. Bring the vinegar, sugar, honey, and 4 cups of water to a boil in a pot. Pour the hot liquid over the cucumbers, leaving ½in (13mm) headspace. Cover the jars with sterilized self-sealing lids and jar rings.

4. Fill a large pot halfway up with water and heat it until it is warm. Gently lower the jars into the pot. Add hot water if needed to ensure the jars are covered by about 1in (2.5cm) of water. Heat the water until the temperature is between 180°F (80°C) and 185°F (85°C). Process the cucumbers at this temperature for 30 minutes. Remove the jars from the pot and let cool. Leave the pickles to marinate for at least 1 week before opening.

TIP: The DILL PICKLES will keep for a year. You can vary the flavor by adding chili pepper flakes, curry powder, garlic, or celery seed, for example, or by using different kinds of vinegar, such as cider vinegar.

MAKES 5 JARS
Preparation time:
  25 minutes
Soaking time: 12 hours
Canning time: 30 minutes
Marinating time: 1 week

4½lb (2kg) pickling
  cucumbers
2 tbsp salt
1 onion
2 medium carrots
¼ fresh horseradish root
5 sprigs of tarragon
5 heads of fresh dill
1½ tbsp whole mixed
  pickling spice
4 cups white wine vinegar
3½oz (100g) sugar
1¾oz (50g) honey

YOU WILL ALSO NEED
5 mason jars, each holding
  2 cups (500ml)

Hot dishes
and Bavarian classics

Potato soup with hot dogs

Whether in a biergarten or at home, on cooler days nothing tastes better than a hot soup. This potato soup is delicious with or without sausages and can be served as a first course or a main course.

1. Peel the potatoes and cut them into large cubes. Peel the celery root and carrots and cut them into large pieces. Trim the leek and cut it into slices. Chop the parsley. Peel the onion and chop it coarsely.

2. Heat the oil in a large pot and sauté the onion. Add the potatoes, celery root, carrots, leek, parsley, and bay leaf and sauté briefly with the onion. Pour in the vegetable broth and simmer over low heat for about 15 minutes.

3. Remove the bay leaf and purée the soup. Return the soup to a boil, add the marjoram and the cream, and stir. Reduce the heat. Season the soup with salt, pepper, and nutmeg.

4. Slice the hot dogs into bite-size pieces, stir them into the soup, and heat until warmed through. Ladle the potato soup into bowls and serve.

TIP: If you like, you can add a generous shot of beer to the potato soup at the very end. The hops in the beer gives the soup a slightly bitter, tangy flavor.

SERVES 4
Preparation time:
  40 minutes

1⅓lb (600g) white potatoes,
  such as Russet potatoes
2oz (60g) celery root
2oz (60g) carrots
3oz (90g) leek
4 sprigs of parsley
1 onion
2 tbsp vegetable oil
1 bay leaf
3⅓ cups vegetable broth
1 tsp dried marjoram
7fl oz (200g) heavy cream
salt and pepper
1 pinch of ground nutmeg
4–8 hot dogs

Feast day soup

On public holidays, the menu often includes a hearty beef broth chock-full of festive delicacies, topped with a sprinkling of chives.

MAKES 20 DUMPLINGS
Preparation time: 1 hour

FOR THE SEMOLINA DUMPLINGS
2 cups whole milk
2 tbsp butter
5½oz (150g) semolina
salt and pepper
1 pinch of ground nutmeg
1 bunch of flat-leaf parsley
2 large eggs

FOR THE LIVER DUMPLINGS
4 day-old bread rolls
5fl oz (150ml) whole milk
1 onion
1 tbsp butter
7oz (200g) beef liver,
   skin removed
1 bunch of flat-leaf parsley
2 large eggs
salt and pepper
1 pinch of ground nutmeg
1 tsp dried marjoram
1 tsp zest of 1 organic
   lemon

FOR SERVING
1 recipe beef broth
   (see p. 37)
1 recipe crêpes
   (see p. 99)
1 bunch of chives

1. To make the semolina dumplings, bring the milk and butter to a boil. Add the semolina. Cook for about 5 minutes, stirring constantly, until a ball is formed. Season with salt, pepper, and nutmeg. Let cool a bit. Chop the parsley finely. Add the parsley and eggs to the warm semolina mixture and combine.

2. In a pot, bring salted water to a boil. Using two dessert spoons, cut out about 20 dumplings from the semolina mixture. Poach the dumplings for about 10 minutes and remove them from the water with a slotted spoon.

3. To make the liver dumplings, thinly slice the bread and place the slices into a bowl. Boil the milk, pour it over the bread, stir, and let steep for 15 minutes. Peel the onion and chop it finely. Heat up the butter in a frying pan and sweat the onion. Add the onions to the bread. Chop the liver coarsely and purée it. Chop the parsley finely. Combine the liver, parsley, eggs, and the bread mixture. Season with the salt, pepper, nutmeg, marjoram, and lemon zest.

4. In a pot, bring salted water to a boil. Form dumplings the size of golf balls from the liver mixture. Poach them for about 15 minutes over low heat. Remove them from the water with a slotted spoon.

5. Heat the broth. Roll up the crêpes tightly and cut into thin slices. Chop the chives. Portion out the broth, dumplings, and crêpe slices into soup plates. Scatter chives over top.

Roast chicken

The aroma of roasting chicken alone is enough to make the mouth water. Roast chicken with crisp, golden-brown skin is a favorite of biergarten visitors. Why not roast a chicken yourself and take it with you?

SERVES 4
Preparation time:
   15 minutes
Roasting time: 50 minutes

1 tbsp paprika
1 pinch of cayenne pepper
1 tsp sugar
salt, plus more for the
   baking tray
pepper
1 young roasting
   chicken, oven-ready
   (about 2½lb/1.2kg)
3 sprigs of parsley
1 tbsp butter

1. Preheat the oven to 350°F (180°C). In a small bowl, combine the paprika, cayenne pepper, sugar, salt, and pepper.

2. Sprinkle the seasoning mix over the outside of the chicken and inside the cavity. Place the sprigs of parsley in the cavity along with the butter.

3. Cover the bottom of a baking tray with a layer of salt about ⅓in (1cm) thick. Place a roasting rack on the tray. Place the chicken on the rack. Roast it in the middle of the oven for about 50 minutes until it is done. The skin should be golden-brown and crispy.

4. Carve the chicken into four portions and serve it with Bavarian potato salad (see p. 42).

Roast pork

It only takes 15 minutes to prepare this biergarten classic, and the oven mostly takes care of the rest. All you have to do now is baste, and look forward to that delicious crackling!

1. Preheat the oven to 350°F (180°C). Generously season the meat on all sides with salt, pepper, and caraway seeds, and place it in a roasting pan. Peel the onion and cut it into large cubes. Peel the celery root and carrots and cut them into large pieces. Cut the leek into slices. Place the onion, celery, carrots, leek, and parsley in the roasting pan.

2. Pour about 1 cup of water into the roasting pan. Roast the pork in the middle of the oven for about 2 hours. Baste the meat with the juices every 15 minutes. Keep an eye on the temperature and, if the crackling becomes too dark or is not dark enough, reduce or raise the temperature as needed. Toward the end of the cooking time, pour the beer over the top of the pork. If there is not a lot of liquid left in the pan, add some water.

3. Remove the pork from the roasting pan and let it rest while you make the sauce. To make the gravy, pour the pan juices through a fine-meshed sieve into a pot. Let the liquid to stand for a moment. Carefully skim off the fat, leaving just the juices. Bring the juices back to a boil.

4. Carve the roast pork into thick slices. Serve the sauce on the side. Slaw (see p. 49) goes very well with roast pork.

VARIATION: To make pork hocks with crackling, ask the butcher to score the skin of two pork hocks. Roast the hocks as described above. Carve each in half lengthwise to make four portions, and serve.

SERVES 4
Preparation time:
   15 minutes
Roasting time: 2 hours

2.2lb (1kg) pork shoulder
   with skin (ask the
   butcher to score the
   pork skin for you)
salt and pepper
1 tbsp caraway seeds
1 onion
2oz (60g) celery root
2oz (60g) carrots
3oz (90g) leek
4 sprigs of parsley
2 cups dark beer

Schnitzel with pan-fried potatoes

An authentic Wiener schnitzel is made from thinly sliced top round veal, but schnitzels made from pork or turkey also taste delicious.

SERVES 4
Preparation time:
40 minutes
Cooling time: 1 hour

FOR THE PAN-FRIED POTATOES
1¾lb (800g) yellow
potatoes, such as Yukon
Gold (or boiled potatoes
left over from the day
before)
salt
2 onions
2 tbsp vegetable oil
pepper

FOR THE SCHNITZELS
4 thinly cut boneless top
round veal cutlets
(5½oz/150g each)
salt and pepper
2 large eggs
flour, for breading
bread crumbs, for breading
butter, for frying
1 lemon, quartered

1. To make the pan-fried potatoes, boil the potatoes in salted water for about 20 minutes or until done. Drain, let the steam evaporate, and peel. Leave the potatoes to cool for about an hour, then cut them into slices.

2. Preheat the oven to 175°F (80°C). Peel the onions and slice them into rings. Heat the oil in a very large frying pan. Add the potatoes and onions. Fry them over high heat for about 10 minutes until they are golden-brown, turning often. Season to taste with salt and pepper and keep warm in the oven.

3. Flatten the veal cutlets with a meat pounder until they are each about ⅛in (3mm) thick. Season them with salt and pepper. Beat the eggs in a soup plate. Place the flour and the bread crumbs on separate plates. Bread each cutlet by dipping each side of it into the flour, eggs, and bread crumbs. Shake off any excess flour and bread crumbs.

4. In one large or two small frying pans, heat enough butter so the schnitzels can float in it. Fry the schnitzels on one side until they are golden-brown, gently shaking the frying pan so the butter flows over them. Turn over the schnitzels, reduce the heat, and fry until the other side is golden-brown. Drain the schnitzels on paper towels. Serve them with pan-fried potatoes and lemon wedges.

Spare ribs with barbecue sauce

A rack of grilled spare ribs makes for a simple, yet very tasty, dish that goes extremely well with beer.

1. In a large pot, bring a generous amount of salted water to a boil. Lower the pork racks into the water, reduce the heat, and simmer them for about 1 hour. They should be covered with water throughout, so add water if needed.

2. While the pork racks are simmering, prepare the sauce. Peel and finely chop the onion and ginger. Finely chop the chili pepper. Heat up the oil in a small pot, add the onion, ginger, and chili pepper, and sauté. Deglaze with beer and boil the liquid until it is reduced by about half. Stir in the ketchup, orange peel, orange juice, soy sauce, and honey, and cook until the sauce has thickened. Purée the sauce. Reserve some of the sauce in a separate dish to use as a dip for the spare ribs.

3. Preheat the charcoal grill or the oven grill. Remove the pork racks from the water. Brush the racks all over with the sauce. Grill the racks for about 10 minutes on each side until they are crispy on the outside. While you are grilling, brush the racks with the sauce again.

4. Cut between the ribs with a large, sharp knife to make single ribs. Serve with the reserved barbecue sauce, beer bread (see p. 56), and slaw (see p. 49).

VARIATION: To make CHICKEN WINGS, coat chicken wings with the barbeque sauce and grill them for about 7 minutes on each side. Wings will burn quickly over a hot grill, so cook them on a cooler section of the grill or in a grill basket.

SERVES 4
Preparation time:
  40 minutes
Cooking time:
  · 1 hour 45 minutes

FOR THE SPARE RIBS
salt
4 racks of meaty pork ribs
  (1⅓lb/600g each)

FOR THE SAUCE
1 onion
1 walnut-sized piece
  of ginger
1 red chili pepper
1 tbsp vegetable oil
1 cup beer
9oz (250g) ketchup
zest of ½ an organic orange
freshly squeezed juice
  of 1 orange
4 tbsp soy sauce
2 tbsp honey

YOU WILL ALSO NEED
a charcoal grill

Beer goulash

In Bavaria, beer isn't just the national drink—it's also a popular cooking ingredient. Here it lends flavor and subtle seasoning to this gently simmered goulash. All you need with it is a slice of fresh, crusty bread and a freshly poured glass of beer.

SERVES 4
Preparation time:
   35 minutes
Cooking time: 1 hour
   30 minutes

2.2lb (1kg) onions
vegetable oil, for frying
2.2lb (1kg) beef stewing
   meat
1 tbsp tomato paste
1 tbsp paprika
1 cup beer
3½ cups water
1⅓lb (600g) yellow
   potatoes, such as
   Yukon Gold
salt and pepper
1 tsp dried marjoram
1 tsp caraway seeds
zest of 1 organic lemon

1. Peel the onions and chop them finely. Heat some oil in a large pot and sauté the onions. Add the beef and fry it for about 10 minutes until the juices it releases have completely boiled away.

2. Stir in the tomato paste. Sprinkle the paprika over the meat. Pour in the beer and deglaze, then add 3½ cups of water. Bring everything to a boil, reduce the heat, and gently simmer the goulash for about 70 minutes, stirring now and then. Season with the salt, pepper, marjoram, caraway seeds, and lemon zest.

3. Peel the potatoes and cut them into large cubes. Add them to the stew, and cook for 20 minutes more until they are done. Serve with beer bread (see p. 56).

Steak and onions

In a biergarten on a sunny day, a tender grilled steak smothered with fried onions tastes heavenly. But this dish also turns out well made at home. By the time the grill is piping hot, the steak is almost ready.

1. Preheat a charcoal grill. Peel the onions and cut them into rings. Combine the flour and paprika in a soup plate. Heat up frying oil in a pot.

2. Dredge the onion rings in the flour and paprika, place them into a sieve, and shake off the excess flour. Working in batches, fry the onion rings in the hot oil for 3 minutes until they are crisp. Remove them from the oil and drain on paper towels.

3. Coarsely crush the mixed peppercorns in a mortar. Season the steaks with salt and crushed pepper.

4. Place the steaks on the hot grill and grill about 5 minutes for medium rare, about 10 minutes for well-done. Only turn the steaks once.

5. Just before serving, turn the steaks again. Serve them immediately on four plates and place the fried onions on top. Traditionally, pan-fried potatoes (see p. 80) are served with this steak.

TIP: Steak also turns out well when cooked in a frying pan. Heat up some oil in a large frying pan. Fry the steaks on one side at high heat. Turn them over, reduce the heat, and fry for about 5 minutes for medium rare or 10 minutes for well-done. Flip the steaks again. Immediately remove them from the frying pan and top them with the fried onions. Deglaze the frying pan with beer, bring the liquid to a boil, and serve as a sauce with the steak.

SERVES 4
Preparation time:
    25 minutes

2 onions
3 tbsp all-purpose flour
1 tsp paprika
vegetable oil, for frying
4 tsp mixed peppercorns
4 strip loin steaks
    (7½oz/200g each)
salt

YOU WILL ALSO NEED
a charcoal grill

Roast duck with plums

When fall comes, appetite for hearty dishes increases, such as for this roast duck with a spiced plum sauce. A classic variation on this recipe is roast duck with apples, seasoned with marjoram.

SERVES 4–6

Preparation time:
40 minutes
Roasting time: 2 hours

1 duck, oven-ready
(about 5½lb/2.5kg)
salt and pepper
4 onions
1 cinnamon stick
4 cloves
4 sprigs of thyme
1¾lb (800g) fresh plums
(ideally Italian plums,
also called prune plums)

1. Preheat the oven to 350°F (180°C). Season the duck inside and out with salt and pepper. Place it in a roasting pan. Pour about 1 cup of water into the pan. Roast the duck in the middle of the oven for 2 hours. Baste every 15 minutes with the juices. Add some water to the pan, as needed. If the duck looks too dark, reduce the heat. If it looks too light, increase the heat.

2. About 1 hour before the end of the cooking time, peel the onions and cut them into wedges. Add the onions, cinnamon stick, cloves, and thyme to the roasting pan.

3. Cut the plums in half and remove the pits. About 15 minutes before the end of the roasting time, scatter the plums around the duck in the roasting pan.

4. Remove the duck from the roasting pan and keep warm. Using a slotted spoon, scoop out the plums and onions. Set aside. To make the sauce, pour the pan juices through a fine-meshed sieve into a pot. Let the liquid stand for a moment. Carefully skim off the fat, leaving just the juices. Return the juices to a simmer. Add the plums and onion, and heat until they are just warmed through.

5. Carve the duck into portions. Serve the duck with the plum sauce on the side and potato noodles (see p. 117).

Hamburger patties

Whether you serve them warm or cold, with potato salad, pasta salad, pan-fried potatoes, or simply in a bun with mustard, everyone loves hamburger patties. Bite-size versions, with crunchy Daikon radish and open-faced chive sandwiches, taste delicious with beer.

1. Place the bread in a bowl, add about ¼ cup of water, and let stand for about 30 minutes. Remove the bread from the water and squeeze it to expel as much of the water as possible. Purée the bread.

2. Peel the onion and chop it finely. Melt the butter in a frying pan and sauté the onion. Set aside to cool. Chop the parsley finely.

3. Place the ground meat, bread, onion, parsley, egg, and mustard into a bowl and combine thoroughly. Season the meat with salt, pepper, paprika, and marjoram. Shape the ground meat mixture into 8 hamburger patties.

4. Heat up some oil in a large frying pan. Sear the hamburgers on each side. Reduce the heat, then fry the hamburgers for about 5 minutes on each side until they are cooked through. Serve with potato salad (see p. 42) and homemade mustard (see p. 29).

TIP: If you use only ground beef instead of ground beef and pork, the meat patties will have a looser texture. They will also be leaner.

SERVES 4
Preparation time:
    25 minutes
Soaking time: 30 minutes

1 day-old bread roll
1 onion
1 tbsp butter
1 bunch of flat-leaf parsley
1 lb 2 oz (500g) mixed
    ground meat
    (beef and pork)
1 large egg
1 tbsp mustard
salt and pepper
3 tsp paprika
1 tsp dried marjoram
vegetable oil, for frying

Pork and egg sandwich

Smoked pork loin topped with fried egg is practically an entire meal packed into one bun. If you serve it at a party, part of the fun for guests is stacking the sandwich just the way they want it.

SERVES 4
Preparation time:
  25 minutes

2 tomatoes
4 dill pickles (see p. 69)
1 red onion
4 pretzel rolls
vegetable oil, for frying
4 boneless smoked pork
  loin chops, about
  3½oz (100g) each
4 eggs
salt and pepper
4 tbsp sweet mustard
  (see p. 29)
1 handful of lettuce leaves

YOU WILL ALSO NEED
wooden skewers to hold
  everything together

1. Preheat the oven to 350°F (180°C). Thinly slice the tomatoes and dill pickles. Peel the onion and slice it into rings. Cut the bread rolls in half and place them in the middle of the oven to bake for about 5 minutes.

2. Heat up some oil in two large frying pans. In one frying pan, fry the pork loin chops for about 5 minutes on each side until they are browned and heated through.

3. Break the eggs into the second frying pan. Fry them over low heat for 2–3 minutes until the whites have just set. Flip the eggs and fry them for another 2–3 minutes. Season the eggs to taste with salt and pepper.

4. Spread the sweet mustard over both halves of each roll and top with lettuce leaves. On the bottom half of each roll, place a pork loin chop, and top it with a fried egg. Add a layer of tomato and cucumbers and then an onion ring. Replace the top halves of the rolls. Insert wooden skewers to hold the sandwiches together. Serve them immediately, while they are still hot. If you like, you can serve roast potato wedges (see p. 100) on the side.

VARIATION: This sandwich also can be made with thick slices of a freshly baked Bavarian luncheon meat called "Leberkaese." It is very popular in Bavaria. There are butchers elsewhere specializing in German products who make and sell "Leberkaese," so ask around if you would like to find a source for this product.

Pork sausages with sauerkraut

Pork sausages are a Munich specialty. They are generally made by hand from coarsely ground pork and are seasoned with salt, pepper, lemon zest, mace, and marjoram. They are about 6in (15cm) long and usually come in pairs. A regular serving is two pairs, or four sausages.

1. To prepare the sauerkraut, peel the onion and slice it into rings. Heat up the oil in a pot, add the onion, and sauté it. Add the sauerkraut and the vegetable broth. Stir in the peppercorns, juniper berries, clove, bay leaf, and sugar, and season with salt. Reduce the heat and simmer the sauerkraut for about 20 minutes.

2. To fry the sausages, heat up some oil in a large frying pan. Fry the sausages for about 10 minutes on each side until they are golden-brown in color.

3. Portion out the sauerkraut and the pork sausages onto four plates. Serve with mustard on the side.

TIP: Other types of sausages also taste very good with sauerkraut. When the weather permits, cook the sausages on a charcoal grill.

SERVES 4
Preparation time:
    25 minutes

FOR THE SAUERKRAUT
1 onion
1 tbsp vegetable oil
1lb 2oz (500g) sauerkraut
⅓ cup (300ml) vegetable
    broth
½ tsp black peppercorns
½ tsp juniper berries
1 clove
1 bay leaf
1 pinch of sugar
salt

FOR THE SAUSAGES
vegetable oil, for frying
16 pork sausages
mustard (see p. 29),
    for serving

Mushroom goulash with pretzel dumplings

When the summer slowly begins to wane in Bavaria, the mushroom-gathering season starts. This is the time when biergartens often feature chanterelle mushrooms—an incomparable delicacy—on their menus.

SERVES 4
Preparation time: 1 hour

FOR THE DUMPLINGS
1 recipe bread dumplings (see p. 41) made with 6 day-old pretzels (see p. 55) or store-bought pretzels instead of bread

FOR THE MUSHROOMS
1 onion
1 bunch of flat-leaf parsley
clarified butter for frying
1lb 2oz (500g) chanterelle mushrooms
3½fl oz (100ml) white wine
salt and pepper
14fl oz (400g) heavy cream

1. To make the pretzel dumplings, make the bread dumplings as described on page 41 using fresh pretzels instead of bread.

2. To make the mushroom goulash, peel the onion and chop it finely. Chop the parsley finely.

3. Heat up some clarified butter in a large frying pan, add the diced onion, and sauté. Add the chanterelle mushrooms and sauté them for about 5 minutes over high heat. Deglaze the frying pan with white wine, then simmer until the wine has evaporated. Season the mushrooms with salt and pepper. Pour in the cream, return to a boil, and simmer for about 5 minutes until the sauce is thick and creamy.

4. Portion out the mushroom goulash onto four plates. Place one dumpling on each plate. Garnish with parsley and serve.

TIP: Pretzel dumplings are made in the same way as bread dumplings, but they are more flavorful. Bread dumplings also go well with this dish.

Crêpes filled with sauerkraut

These filled crêpes sound unusual but taste delicious. They are equally good warm or cold, and are great for eating outdoors.

1. To make the crêpes, chop the parsley and chives finely. Combine the flour, salt, pepper, and nutmeg in a bowl. Add the milk and eggs, and mix to make a batter that is thick enough to coat the back of a spoon. Stir in the parsley and chives.

2. Heat up some oil in a frying pan. Using a ladle, evenly coat the bottom of the frying pan with the batter. Fry the crêpe over moderate heat until it is golden-brown underneath, turn it gently, and brown the other side. Remove the crêpe from the frying pan. Repeat to make the rest of the crêpes. The batter should yield about four to 8 crêpes, depending on the size of the frying pan.

3. Preheat the oven to 350°F (180°C). Butter an ovenproof casserole dish.

4. To fill the crêpes, spread each crêpe evenly with the sauerkraut. Roll up the crêpes, cut them into thick pieces, and stand them upright in the dish. Place one knob of butter on each piece and bake them in the middle of the oven for between 20 and 35 minutes, depending on the size and thickness of the crêpes. Serve with sour cream.

TIP: These crêpes are satisfyingly filling when served as a main dish. Served in smaller pieces, they make a great first course or finger food. Slice the filled crêpes into thin pieces. Use toothpicks to hold them together. Serve the sour cream on the side as a dip.

SERVES 4
Preparation time:
    45 minutes
Baking time: 20–35 minutes

FOR THE PANCAKES
1 bunch of flat-leaf parsley
1 bunch of chives
14oz (400g) all-purpose
    flour
salt and pepper
1 pinch of ground nutmeg
2½ cups (600ml) whole
    milk
4 eggs
vegetable oil, for frying
butter, for the ovenproof
    casserole dish

FOR THE FILLING
1 recipe sauerkraut,
    lukewarm (see p. 95)
2 tbsp butter
7oz (200g) sour cream,
    for serving

Roast potato wedges with two dips

Freshly cut potato wedges roasted in the oven and served with these two dips are a real treat. Children may even prefer them to their normally beloved French fries!

SERVES 4
Preparation time:
25 minutes
Roasting time: 20 minutes

FOR THE POTATO WEDGES
1¾lb (800g) yellow
  potatoes, such as
  Yukon Gold
salt and freshly ground
  black pepper
1 tsp sugar
1 tbsp paprika
1 tbsp curry powder
1 pinch of cayenne pepper
olive oil

FOR THE AVOCADO DIP
2 ripe avocados
1 tomato
freshly squeezed juice of
  ½ a lemon
salt and freshly ground
  black pepper

FOR THE SOUR CREAM DIP
7oz (200g) sour cream
1 squeeze of lemon juice
salt and freshly ground
  black pepper

1. To make the potato wedges, preheat the oven to 400°F (200°C). Wash the potatoes but do not peel them. Cut the potatoes into wedges and arrange them on a baking tray.

2. Mix together the salt, pepper, sugar, paprika, curry powder, and cayenne pepper. Sprinkle the seasoning over the potato wedges and generously drizzle olive oil over them. Place the potatoes in the middle of the oven. Bake them for about 20 minutes, turning them now and then, until they are golden-brown and crisp.

3. To make the avocado dip, slice the avocado in half lengthwise, remove the stone, and scoop out the avocado flesh. Mash the avocado with a fork until smooth. Finely dice the tomato. Stir the tomato and lemon juice into the mashed avocado. Season to taste with salt and pepper.

4. To make the sour cream dip, stir together the sour cream and lemon juice. Season with salt and pepper. Remove the roasted potato wedges from the oven, portion out on plates, and serve the dips on the side.

TIP: Ketchup flavored with curry is also a great dip to serve with these potatoes. Place ½ cup of ketchup in a bowl, add some curry powder and cayenne pepper, and stir.

Tyrolean hash with fried eggs

Do you have some leftover roast pork? And are there a few potatoes in the pantry? How about a few eggs? And onions? This is a recipe that uses up leftovers in the most delicious way imaginable.

1. Wash the potatoes and boil them in salted water for about 20 minutes or until they are done. Drain, let the steam evaporate briefly, and peel. Leave the potatoes to cool for about 1 hour, then cut them into slices.

2. Peel the onions and slice them into rings. Cut the bacon into narrow strips. Cut the roast pork into small cubes.

3. Heat up 2 tablespoons of oil in one large frying pan or two small ones. Place the potatoes, onions, bacon, and roast pork in the frying pan. Fry over high heat for about 10 minutes until the ingredients are golden-brown in color, turning often. Season with salt, pepper, marjoram, and caraway seeds.

4. Using another frying pan, heat up 1 tablespoon of oil. Break the eggs gently into the frying pan and fry them for about 5 minutes over low heat until the whites have set. Season the eggs with pepper and paprika.

5. Portion out the hash onto four plates. Top each plate with an egg. Serve with dill pickles and salt for the eggs.

TIP: For an even quicker method, make the hash with scrambled eggs. Whisk together the eggs with salt, pepper, and paprika. When the potatoes are golden-brown, turn the heat down to low. Pour the eggs over the potatoes and cook them until they are set. Serve immediately. You can also fry sliced dumplings and cooked vegetables (such as carrots, beans, peas, and cauliflower) with the potatoes.

SERVES 4
Preparation time:
40 minutes
Cooling time: 1 hour

1¾lb (800g) yellow potatoes, such as Yukon Gold (or leftover boiled potatoes)
salt
2 onions
3½oz (100g) marbled smoked bacon
¾lb (350g) cold roast pork (see p. 79)
3 tbsp vegetable oil
pepper
1 tsp dried marjoram
½ tsp caraway seeds
4 eggs
1 tsp paprika
4 dill pickles (see p. 69)

Cheese spaetzle

Both in the biergarten and at home, a plate of cheese spaetzle is always a pleasure to eat. Swiss cheese makes this dish nice and creamy, and fried onions add even more flavor and a rustic touch.

SERVES 4

Preparation time:
  40 minutes

salt
9oz (250g) all-purpose flour
4½oz (125g) semolina
3 eggs
pepper
1 pinch of ground nutmeg
5½oz (150g) Gruyère
  cheese, freshly grated
2 onions
1 bunch of chives
1 tbsp butter, plus more
  for the ovenproof
  casserole dish

YOU WILL ALSO NEED

a spaetzle maker (see tip)

1. Place the oven rack in the middle of the oven. Preheat the oven to 350°F (180°C). Butter an ovenproof casserole dish. In a tall pot, bring a large quantity of salted water to a boil.

2. Mix the flour and semolina in a bowl. Add the eggs and about 7fl oz (200ml) of cold water. Season with salt, pepper, and nutmeg. Beat the mixture, ideally by hand, until the dough is thick yet drips slowly off a cooking spoon. Beat for 5 minutes more until small bubbles form.

3. Ladle a portion of dough into the spaetzle maker and press it into the boiling water. Once the spaetzle float up to the surface, remove them with a slotted spoon. Place a layer of spaetzle on the bottom of the casserole dish and top with a layer of grated cheese. Return the dish to the oven to keep warm. Repeat, alternating layers, until the dough and Gruyère cheese are used up.

4. Peel the onions and cut them into rings. Wash the chives and chop them finely. Melt the butter in a frying pan and sauté the onions until they are golden-brown.

5. Place the sautéed onions on top of the spaetzle. Garnish with the chives and serve immediately. A leafy green salad goes very well with this dish.

TIP: If you don't have a spaetzle maker, press the dough through a potato press or a metal colander that has large draining holes.

Spinach dumplings with Gruyère cheese

1. Leave the spinach to defrost for about 1 hour. Prepare the dumpling mixture as described on page 41 from the bread rolls, milk, onion, 1 tablespoon butter, eggs, salt, pepper, nutmeg, and spinach. Add a bit of hot milk or bread crumbs, as needed.

2. Bring a large pot of salted water to a boil. Form peach-sized dumplings from the dough. Place them into the boiling water, then return the water to a boil. Gently simmer the dumplings for about 20 minutes.

3. Melt the remaining butter in a small frying pan until it is foamy. Portion out the dumplings, drizzle melted butter over them, and scatter the Gruyère cheese over the top. A mixed salad goes very well with this dish.

SERVES 4

Preparation time:
    35 minutes
Defrosting time: 1 hour

1lb (450g) frozen spinach, chopped
6 day-old bread rolls
3½fl oz (100ml) whole milk
1 onion
5 tbsp butter
2 large eggs
salt and pepper
1 pinch of ground nutmeg
bread crumbs as needed
5½oz (150g) Gruyère cheese, freshly grated

Fried spinach dumplings

1. Peel the onions and cut them into rings. Cut the dumplings into wedges. Whisk together the eggs and cream, and season with salt and pepper.

2. Heat up some clarified butter in one large frying pan or two small ones. Add the onions and dumplings and fry them over high heat for about 10 minutes until they are crispy, stirring often. Turn down the heat. Pour in the eggs and let them set. Stir everything again thoroughly. Serve with a mixed salad.

TIP: If you would like to add meat, slice 5½oz (150g) of smoked bacon into thin strips and fry it together with the dumplings and onions.

SERVES 4

Preparation time:
    30 minutes

2 onions
1 recipe spinach dumplings, cooled (or left over from the day before)
4 large eggs
3½fl oz (100g) heavy cream
salt and pepper
clarified butter, for frying

Potato pancakes with applesauce

SERVES 4
Preparation time:
  45 minutes

FOR THE APPLESAUCE
2.2lb (1kg) apples
3 tbsp elderflower syrup
peel from an organic lemon
  (2in/5cm long)
3½fl oz (100ml) apple juice

FOR THE POTATO PANCAKES
1¾lb (800g) white potatoes,
  such as Russet potatoes
2 large eggs
salt and pepper
1 pinch of ground nutmeg
vegetable oil, for frying

1. To make the applesauce, peel, quarter, and core the apples. Cut the apple quarters into large pieces and place them in a pot. Add the elderflower syrup, lemon peel, and apple juice. Cook the apples for about 20 minutes until they are soft, stirring now and then.

2. Fish out the lemon peel and thoroughly mash the apples with a potato masher. Leave the applesauce to cool.

3. To make the potato pancakes, first peel the potatoes. Coarsely grate half of the potatoes, then finely grate the other half. Place the potatoes in a sieve set over a bowl and press down on them firmly to squeeze out the liquid. Set aside to drain for about 10 minutes.

4. Carefully pour out the potato liquid from the bowl, leaving the starch that has filtered to the bottom of the bowl behind. Combine the potatoes, potato starch, and eggs, and season with salt, pepper, and nutmeg.

5. Heat up some oil in a large frying pan. For each pancake, place a heaped tablespoon of the potato mixture into the frying pan and flatten it with the back of the spoon. Fry the potato pancakes on each side for about 5 minutes until they are golden-brown and crispy. Place them on paper towels to drain. Serve with applesauce.

TIP: Do you prefer the savory to the sweet? Sauerkraut (see p. 95) goes well with potato pancakes and, even tastier, so does gravlax made from salmon trout fillet and served with a dollop of sour cream.

Pan-fried pasta

For many biergarten visitors, cooked pasta, fried in the pan with ham until it is crispy, is a welcome alternative to heavy meat dishes. This classic dish is quickly prepared at home.

1. Cook the pasta in boiling salted water according to the directions on the package until the pasta is cooked but still firm to the bite. Pour it into a colander, rinse with cold water, and let drain.

2. Cut the ham into cubes $\frac{1}{3}$in (1cm) in size. Chop the chives finely. Whisk together the eggs and cream. Season with salt and pepper.

3. Heat up some clarified butter in one large or two small frying pans. Add the pasta and ham and fry them over high heat for about 5 minutes, stirring constantly, until the pasta and ham are crispy. Season with salt, pepper, and nutmeg. Lower the heat, pour in the eggs, and cook until the eggs are set.

4. Sprinkle the pasta and ham with the chives. Stir well and serve. A mixed salad goes well with this dish.

TIP: This PAN-FRIED PASTA recipe can be turned into a vegetarian dish in a flash. Just use thin slices of zucchini instead of ham, and fresh thyme instead of chives.

SERVES 4
Preparation time:
   25 minutes

14oz (400g) short pasta
   such as rotini, macaroni,
   or bows
salt
5½oz (150g) cooked ham,
   sliced $\frac{1}{3}$in (1cm) thick
1 bunch of chives
6 eggs
3½fl oz (100g) heavy cream
pepper
1 pinch of ground nutmeg
clarified butter, for frying

Taking your children to biergartens

Children love going to biergartens; almost all biergartens provide plenty of room to run around in, great playgrounds, and a huge choice of playmates. And of course, along with beer, there is also soda and apple juice mixed with sparkling water on offer. But the dishes selected for the picnic basket also have to be just right so the little ones are happy and the parents can just sit back and relax. Children are sure to enjoy the following dishes:

Baked potatoes with salmon and ham

SERVES 4
Preparation time:
   20 minutes
Baking time: 1 hour

8–12 large white potatoes,
   such as Russet potatoes
1 bunch of flat-leaf parsley
1 bunch of arugula
1 bunch of chives
1lb 10z (750g) quark
   (40% fat) or sour
   cream (40% fat)
freshly squeezed juice
   of ½ a lemon
1 dash of Worcestershire
   sauce
salt and pepper
5½oz (150g) dry cured ham,
   such as prosciutto
5½oz (150g) smoked
   salmon

1. Preheat the oven to 350°F (180°C). Scrub the potatoes thoroughly, prick them, and wrap each one in a sheet of aluminum foil. Place the potatoes on an oven rack in the middle of the oven and bake them for about 1 hour until they are done.

2. Wash the parsley and chives and chop them finely. Wash the arugula and chop it coarsely. Wash the chives and chop them finely.

3. Mix together the quark or sour cream, lemon juice, and Worcestershire sauce. Stir in the herbs and season the quark or sour cream with salt and pepper. Cut the ham and smoked salmon into strips.

4. Remove the potatoes from the oven. Cut a deep cross into the top of each potato, through the aluminum foil. Using oven gloves and both hands, hold a potato and push toward the middle to open it up.

5. Fill the baked potatoes with the herb mixture and place strips of ham or smoked salmon on the top. Serve baked potatoes as a side dish for steak and onions (see p. 87) or spare ribs (see p. 83), or as a main meal with a mixed salad on the side.

TIP: Instead of ham and smoked salmon, you can use fried diced bacon or fried smoked tofu, chopped eggs, roasted pumpkin seeds, diced tomato, poached or fried shrimp, or pieces of smoked trout fillet. And of course, baked potatoes taste very good with just a herb topping, or sour cream or quark seasoned with salt and pepper.

Potato noodles with sauerkraut

These noodles are often served on the side, or as a dessert with applesauce. With sauerkraut, they make a lovely vegetarian main dish.

1. Boil the potatoes in salted water for about 20 minutes until they are done. Drain them and peel them. While they still are hot, put them through a potato ricer into a bowl. Then let them cool down a bit.

2. On a floured work surface, quickly knead together the potatoes, semolina, flour, and eggs to make a smooth dough. Season with salt, pepper, and nutmeg.

3. Working quickly, roll the dough into logs about 1½in (4cm) thick. Cut the logs into pieces about 2in (5cm) long, and roll the pieces so they taper off to form slightly pointed ends.

4. Heat up a bit of clarified butter in a large frying pan and, turning often, fry the noodles for about 10 minutes until they are golden-brown. Add the sauerkraut to the noodles and mix. Continue to fry the noodles and sauerkraut for about 5 minutes more, or until the sauerkraut is hot. Serve immediately.

TIP: To turn this dish into a non-vegetarian one, slice 5½oz (150g) of marbled smoked bacon into strips. Fry the bacon together with the potato noodles, then add the sauerkraut.

SERVES 4
Preparation time: 1 hour

1¾lb (800g) white potatoes, such as Russet potatoes
salt
3 tbsp semolina
3 tbsp all-purpose flour, plus more for the work surface
2 large eggs
pepper
1 pinch of ground nutmeg
clarified butter, for frying
1 recipe sauerkraut (see p. 95)

YOU WILL ALSO NEED
a potato ricer

A short breviary of beer

It may not come as a surprise that the German beer-drinking record is held by Bavarians. Each year, on average, a Bavarian drinks an impressive 215 liters (in 2013) of beer—and not just the well known Pilsener, either. Read on to find out about the other most important types of beer.

Hell, a light lager, is the classic biergarten drink. It is a bottom-fermented beer, mild and eminently quaffable, with a lower alcohol content than many other German beers. Less strongly hopped than a Pilsener, it is also less bitter. This contributes to its popularity and makes it ideal for mixed beer drinks. Hell is served in liter glasses in biergartens, and one serving is called a "mass" (measure). This light beer goes well with most biergarten food, but especially well with cheese dips.

Weissbier, or wheat beer, is a top-fermented beer. It is a specialty beer made from malted wheat and barley. For a long time, it was purely a Bavarian affair. Over the years, Bavarian brews such as light and dark Weissbier, yeast Weissbier (also called Hefeweizen), and filtered yeast Weissbier (Kristallweizen) have become popular throughout Germany. To this day, most wheat beers come from Bavaria. Weissbier is served in tall, slender, slightly curved glasses that hold half a liter. It is delicious with mild types of cheese, fresh cheese dips, or young Camembert.

Bockbier can be either top or bottom fermented. It is a strong ale with a specific gravity of at least 16 and an alcohol content of 6 percent by volume. **Doppelbockbier** has a specific gravity of 18 and an alcohol content of more than 7 percent by volume. Since the end of the Middle Ages, it has traditionally been brewed in monasteries, especially during Lent, to make it easier for the monks to deny themselves solid food. Traditionally in Bavaria, the first barrel of bock beer is tapped each year around March 19, Saint Joseph's Day. In the summer, during biergarten season, bock beer is not sold. Strong bock ales go very well with rich desserts, such as apple fritters.

Radler, the beloved shandy made by mixing equal portions of Hell beer and clear, sparkling lemonade together, was created by a Munich local after World War I. He wanted to ensure cyclists ("Radler") could cycle home in a straight line after visiting a biergarten. This drink used to be mixed on the spot as the bartender saw fit. In 1993, after a change to German beer tax law, "Radler" shandy was allowed to be sold pre-mixed in bottles. It is also available by the liter in biergartens and is called a "Radlermass," "Radler" for short.

Russ, or Russn, is, like the "Radler," a shandy. It is made by mixing together equal portions of Weissbier and clear, sparkling lemonade. Its name is short for "Russ'n-Mass" (Russian Mass). Apparently it was invented during the time of the short-lived Munich Soviet Republic. The revolutionaries were called "Russ'n" (Russians) by the locals, and this became the name of the thirst-quenching drink.

Tomato and basil quiche tarts

These easy-to-eat quiches, with their firm bases and moist filling, taste good both warm and cold. They are ideal for the picnic basket.

MAKES 6 SMALL QUICHES
Preparation time:
    40 minutes
Resting time: 30 minutes
Baking time: 35 minutes

FOR THE PASTRY
3½oz (100g) cold butter
7oz (200g) all-purpose flour,
    plus more for the work
    surface
salt

FOR THE TOPPING
1¾lb (800g) large red
    cherry tomatoes
salt and pepper
9oz (250g) ricotta cheese
200 g heavy cream
4 eggs
olive oil, for drizzling
5½oz (150g) freshly grated
    Gruyère cheese
1 bunch of fresh basil

YOU WILL ALSO NEED
6 mini quiche dishes (about
    6in/15cm in diameter)
2.2lb (1kg) pie weights
    (ceramic baking beans or
    dried pulses), for blind
    baking

1. To make the pastry, cut the butter into cubes. Combine the flour, salt, cubes of butter, and about 3½fl oz (100ml) of cold water. Knead into a smooth dough. Gather the dough into a ball, wrap it in plastic wrap, and leave it to rest in the refrigerator for 30 minutes.

2. Preheat the oven to 350°F (180°C). Roll out the dough on a floured work surface. Cut out six circles large enough to line a tart tin from the dough. Line the tart dishes with the dough. Prick the dough with the tines of a fork. Cut out six circles of parchment paper to fit the tart tins. Line the pastry with the parchment paper and fill with the pie weights. Bake the pastry shells in the middle of the oven for about 10 minutes. Take them out of the oven and carefully remove the parchment paper and pie weights.

3. Cut the tomatoes in half. Distribute them over the tart shell bases, cut side up, and season them with salt and pepper. Whisk together the ricotta, cream, and eggs, and season to taste with salt and pepper. Pour the mixture around the tomatoes.

4. Bake the quiches in the middle of the oven for about 25 minutes. When they are done, drizzle some olive oil over each one. Then sprinkle Gruyère cheese over the top, followed by a scattering of fresh basil leaves.

Flammkuchen with onions and bacon

1. Sift the flour into a large mixing bowl. Make a deep well in the middle. Crumble the yeast into the well. Add the sugar and some lukewarm water. Stirring in the well, incorporate some flour into the liquid. Cover the bowl and leave it in a warm place for about 15 minutes.

2. Add the salt, oil, and 7fl oz (200ml) of lukewarm water to the bowl. Using your fingers, mix to form a dough. Turn out the dough onto a floured work surface. Using your hands, knead vigorously. Cover and let rise for 1 hour.

3. While the dough is rising, peel the onions and slice them into thin rings. Dice the bacon finely.

4. Heat the butter in a frying pan, add the bacon, and sauté. Drain the bacon on paper towels. Sauté the onions in the bacon fat for about 5 minutes, remove them from the heat, and let cool. Whisk together the sour cream and egg yolk, and season with salt, pepper, and nutmeg.

5. Preheat the oven to 425°F (220°C). Line a baking tray with parchment paper. Knead the dough again. Divide it into 8 portions. Roll out each portion into a thin oval tart.

6. Place the tarts on the baking tray and spread them with sour cream. Place onions and bacon on top, followed by a sprinkling of caraway seeds. Bake the tarts in the middle of the oven for about 20 minutes until they are crisp.

TIP: To make a vegetarian version, top the sour cream with thinly sliced tomatoes and zucchini. Season with salt and pepper, sprinkle thyme and grated Gruyère over the top, and bake as above.

TO MAKE 8 TARTS
Preparation time:
    45 minutes
Rising time: 1 hour
    15 minutes
Baking time: 20 minutes

FOR THE DOUGH
5½oz (150g) all-purpose
    flour, plus more for the
    work surface
5½oz (150g) dark rye flour
¾oz (20g) yeast cake
    or 1 tsp active dry yeast
1 pinch of sugar
salt
1 tbsp vegetable oil

FOR THE TOPPING
3 onions
5½oz (150g) marbled
    smoked bacon, such as
    pancetta
1 tbsp clarified butter
7oz (200g) sour cream
1 large egg yolk
salt and pepper
1 pinch of ground nutmeg
1 tsp caraway seeds

Sweet treats

Apple strudel pastries

MAKES 8
Preparation time: 1 hour
Rising time: 30 minutes
Baking time: 25 minutes

FOR THE STRUDEL DOUGH
9oz (250g) all-purpose flour,
   plus more for the work
   surface
salt
1 large egg
2 tbsp vegetable oil

FOR THE FILLING
3 tbsp raisins
2.2lb (1kg) apples
3 tbsp whole hazelnuts
2 tbsp sugar
1 tsp cinnamon
3 tbsp butter
bread crumbs,
   for sprinkling
confectioner's sugar,
   for dusting

1. Sift together the flour and salt. Add the egg, oil, and about 5fl oz (150ml) of lukewarm water. Turn out the flour mixture onto a floured work surface. Using your hands, knead the mixture to make a moderately firm dough. Rinse a bowl with warm water, invert it over the dough, and let stand for about 30 minutes.

2. Soak the raisins in water. Peel the apples, cut them into eights, and remove the cores. Finely chop the apples and place them in a bowl. Coarsely chop the hazelnuts. Drain the raisins and stir them into the diced apples along with the hazelnuts, sugar, and cinnamon.

3. Preheat the oven to 350°F (180°C). Line a baking tray with parchment paper. Place the dough on the floured work surface and knead vigorously. Divide the dough into four portions. Roll out one portion. Dust a clean kitchen towel with flour and place the dough on it. Using your hands, stretch the dough out as thinly as possible to form a rectangle about 12 x 20in (30 x 50cm) in size.

4. Melt the butter. Brush the dough with the butter and scatter bread crumbs sparsely over the top. Spread a quarter of the apples over the top, leaving a gap between the apples and the edge of the dough of about 1in (3cm). Using the kitchen towel, roll up the dough to form a long strudel. Cut it in half and form snail-shaped pastries from each half. Place the pastries on the baking tray. Repeat with the rest of the dough.

5. Brush the pastries with melted butter. Bake them in the middle of the oven for about 25 minutes. Dust with confectioner's sugar and serve. Vanilla ice cream or vanilla custard go very well with these pastries.

Poppy seed and apricot strudel

Strudel filled with quark or yogurt and sour cream is a very popular dish in Bavaria. The classic Bavarian filling contains raisins. Here, apricots and poppy seed are used instead, for a taste of summer.

1. Prepare the dough as described on page 126 and let it stand for 30 minutes. Cut the apricots in half, remove the pits, and cut the fruit into wedges. Separate the eggs. In a bowl, whip the egg whites until they form stiff peaks.

2. Set aside 3 tablespoons of the butter. Place the remaining butter in a bowl, add the sugar and vanilla, and beat until frothy. Beat in the egg yolks one at a time. Stir in the quark or yogurt and sour cream, the poppy seed, lemon zest, and apricots. Fold the mixture into the egg whites.

3. Preheat the oven to 350°F (180°C). Generously butter a roasting pan. Place the dough on a floured work surface and knead vigorously. Roll out the dough. Place it on top of a clean kitchen towel dusted with flour. Using your hands, stretch out the dough as thinly as possible until it forms a rectangle 16x24in (40x60cm) in size.

4. Spread the filling over the dough, leaving a gap along the dough edge of 1in (3cm). Using the kitchen towel, roll up the dough. Fold the ends underneath and place the strudel in the roasting pan. Melt the remaining butter and brush it over the strudel. Bake the strudel in the middle of the oven for about 1 hour.

5. Let the strudel sit for 15 minutes. Then, dust it with confectioner's sugar, cut it into thick slices, and serve.

MAKES 1 STRUDEL (ABOUT 12 SLICES)
Preparation time: 40 minutes
Rising time: 45 minutes
Baking time: 1 hour

1 recipe strudel dough (see p. 126)
1¾lb (800g) apricots
3 large eggs
5½oz (150g) unsalted butter, softened, plus more for the roasting pan
5½oz (150g) sugar
1 package vanilla sugar or 1 tsp pure vanilla extract
1lb 2oz (500g) quark (alternatively, use a thick and creamy, plain, non-fat yogurt)
9oz (250g) quark (40% fat) or sour cream (40% fat)
3½oz (100g) ground poppy seed
zest of 1 organic lemon
confectioner's sugar, for dusting

Bavarian donuts

This beloved Bavarian fried treat tastes best fresh from the frying pan dipped in loads of sugar. Formerly, these donuts were only made on feast days. Today, thankfully, things are more relaxed.

MAKES 10

Preparation time: 1 hour
Rising time:
   1 hour 30 minutes

1 recipe yeast dough
   (see p. 137)
2 egg yolks
flour, for the work surface
vegetable oil, for frying
   (see tip)
sugar

1. Prepare the dough as described on page 137, but knead in the egg yolks. Cover the dough and let it rise in a warm place for 1 hour.

2. Place the dough on a floured work surface and knead vigorously. Divide the dough into 10 portions. Shape the portions into circles about 4in (10cm) in diameter. Place them side by side on a floured work surface and cover with a clean kitchen towel. Let them rest for 15 minutes.

3. Heat up a generous amount of oil in a shallow pot. Place your fingers firmly in the middle of each round of dough to anchor it on the work surface. Stretch the edges of the dough outward until the middle of the donut is flat and there is a raised edge all around of about 1in (3cm).

4. Working in batches, fry the donuts in the hot oil for 2–3 minutes until they are golden-brown. The donuts will curve lightly upward. Carefully turn them over. Drain the hot oil from the middles of the donuts as you do so, so that they remain light in color. Fry the donuts on the other side for 2–3 minutes until golden-brown.

5. Using a slotted spoon, remove the donuts from the oil. Place them on paper towels to drain. While they are still hot, dip the donuts in the sugar and serve immediately.

TIP: Donuts taste even better when fried in two kinds of fat. Use half butter or pork lard, and half vegetable oil or shortening.

Apple fritters with walnut ice cream

The secret to the delicious taste of these fritters lies in the batter, which contains beer. It gives the apple fritters a delicate flavor.

SERVES 4

Preparation time:
  40 minutes

4 cooking apples (such as Granny Smith)
5½oz (150g) all-purpose flour
½ tsp baking powder
1 pinch of salt
5fl oz (150ml) beer
2 large eggs
7fl oz (200g) heavy cream, for serving
4 tbsp sugar
½ tsp ground cinnamon
vegetable oil, for frying
walnut ice cream, for serving

1. Peel and core the apples with an apple corer. Slice the apples horizontally into finger-thick slices.

2. Sift the flour, baking powder, and salt into a bowl. Pour in the beer and stir to form a thick batter. Separate the eggs. Beat the egg whites until they form stiff peaks. Stir the egg yolks into the batter, then fold the batter into the egg whites.

3. Whip the cream until it forms stiff peaks. Mix together the sugar and cinnamon on a plate.

4. Heat up the oil in a shallow pot. Dip the apple slices one at a time into the batter. Let the excess batter drain off. Immediately place the apple slices into the hot oil. Fry the slices for about 5 minutes on each side until golden-brown. Remove from the oil and drain them on paper towels. While they are still hot, dip them in the cinnamon sugar.

5. Portion out the apple fritters onto four plates. Serve hot with the whipped cream and walnut ice cream.

Kaiserschmarrn

The Austrian Emperor Franz Joseph was supposedly fond of this dish. It is a classic in biergartens, mountain huts, and Bavarian restaurants. Eaten as a sweet main course, it makes a filling meal for one. Eaten as a dessert, it makes a treat for many.

SERVES 4
Preparation time:
   30 minutes

4 tbsp raisins
7oz (200g) all-purpose flour
½ tsp baking powder
1 tbsp sugar
1 pinch of salt
7fl oz (200ml) whole milk
4 eggs
clarified unsalted butter,
   for frying
4 tbsp sliced almonds
confectioner's sugar
lingonberry or cranberry
   compote, for serving

1. Soak the raisins in water. Combine the flour, baking powder, sugar, and salt in a bowl. Add the milk and mix to make a thick batter.

2. Separate the eggs. Whip the egg whites until they form stiff peaks. Stir the egg yolks into the batter. Fold the batter into the egg whites.

3. Melt some clarified butter in one large frying pan or two small ones. Pour the batter into the frying pan. Drain the raisins. Sprinkle the raisins and sliced almonds over the batter. Reduce the heat and fry the pancake for about 10 minutes or until it is golden-brown underneath. Cover the frying pan if needed. Carefully turn the pancake over and fry the second side until it, too, is golden-brown.

4. Remove the frying pan from the stove. Using two forks, tear apart the pancake into bite-size pieces. Dust the pieces generously with confectioner's sugar and return the frying pan to the stove. Caramelize the sugar over medium heat, turning the pancake pieces often.

5. Portion out onto four plates and dust with confectioner's sugar. Serve with lingonberry or cranberry compote.

TIP: Kaiserschmarrn also tastes very good when served with applesauce (see p. 108) or plum compote.

Baked dumplings with cherries

Baked yeast dumplings come out of the oven golden-brown and crisp. They taste best in summer when they are prepared with fresh cherries.

1. Sift the flour into a large mixing bowl. Make a deep well in the center. Crumble the yeast into the well and add a pinch of the sugar and some lukewarm water. Stirring in the well, incorporate some flour into the liquid. Cover the bowl with a kitchen towel and let rise in a warm place for about 15 minutes.

2. Melt the butter. Add half of the butter, the remaining milk and sugar, the eggs, and the lemon zest to the bowl. Using your fingers, mix the ingredients to form a dough. Using your hands, knead the dough thoroughly on a floured work surface. Cover the bowl with a kitchen towel. Let the dough rise in a warm place for about 1 hour.

3. To make the filling, remove the stems from the cherries and pit them. Preheat the oven to 350°F (180°C). Generously butter an ovenproof casserole dish.

4. Knead the dough well again and then divide it into 6–12 portions. Flatten each portion slightly and fill it with cherries. Pinch the dough closed and shape it to form tall dumplings. Arrange the dumplings side by side in an ovenproof casserole dish. Pour some milk into the dish and brush the rest of the butter over the dumplings. Bake them in the middle of the oven for about 50 minutes. Dust them with the confectioner's sugar and serve.

VARIATION: For steamed plum dumplings, fill the dumplings with plum compote and steam them. Sprinkle with a mixture of melted butter and ground poppy seed. Dust with confectioner's sugar.

MAKES 6–12 DUMPLINGS
Preparation time:
  45 minutes
Rising time:
  1 hour 15 minutes
Baking time: 50 minutes

FOR THE DOUGH
1lb 2oz (500g) all-purpose flour, plus more for the work surface
¾oz (20g) yeast cake or 1 tsp active dry yeast
2oz (60g) sugar
1 cup whole milk, lukewarm, plus more for baking
3½oz (100g) butter, plus more for the ovenproof casserole dish
2 large eggs
zest of an organic lemon
confectioner's sugar for dusting

FOR THE FILLING
1lb 2oz (500g) cherries

Plum tart with streusel topping

When it is summer, it is time for plum tart. If you can get them, use prune plums, also called Italian plums, for this juicy tart—although almost any plum will be fine.

MAKES 1 BAKING TRAY
Preparation time:
    45 minutes
Rising time:
    1 hour 15 minutes
Baking time: 45 minutes

FOR THE DOUGH
10½oz (300g) all-purpose
    flour, plus more for the
    work surface
¾oz (20g) yeast cake or
    1 tsp active dry yeast
1½oz (40g) sugar
7fl oz (200ml) whole milk,
    lukewarm
3oz (80g) butter
2 large eggs
zest of ½ an organic lemon

FOR THE TOPPING
3⅓lb (1.5kg) fresh plums
bread crumbs,
    for sprinkling
3½oz (100g) all-purpose
    flour
4½oz (125g) sugar
3½oz (100g) ground
    hazelnuts
½ tsp ground cinnamon
1 pinch of salt
3½oz (100g) cold unsalted
    butter

1. Make the yeast dough as described on page 137 in steps 1 and 2 using the dough ingredients on this page.

2. To make the topping, cut the plums in half lengthwise. Make cuts on both ends, open up the plums, and remove the pits, making sure the halves are still attached. There should be four points at each end.

3. Preheat the oven to 350°F (180°C). Line a rimmed baking tray about 16x12x1in (40x30x2.5cm) in size with parchment paper. Turn out the dough onto the floured work surface and knead vigorously. Roll out the dough to fit the baking tray. Place it on the baking tray.

4. Sprinkle a thin layer of bread crumbs onto the dough. In rows, closely pack the plums on top.

5. Combine the flour, sugar, hazelnuts, cinnamon, and salt in a bowl. Cut the butter into cubes and add it to the flour mixture. Knead everything together to create streusel crumbs. Distribute the streusel over the plums. Bake the tart in the middle of the oven for about 45 minutes. Serve with whipped cream.

TIP: Plum tart also tastes good without the streusel topping. When plums are not in season, you can top the yeast dough with apples, apricots, cherries, or just with streusel alone.

Hazelnut yeast braid with a rum glaze

1. Prepare a yeast dough as described in steps 1 and 2 on page 137.

2. Soak the raisins in water. Place the cream in a small pot and bring it to a boil. Stir in the hazelnuts, bread crumbs, sugar, vanilla sugar or vanilla extract, and cinnamon. Remove the mixture from the stove. Drain the raisins and stir them into the hazelnut mixture. Set aside the mixture to cool.

3. Preheat the oven to 350°F (180°C). Line a baking tray with parchment paper. Turn out the dough onto the floured work surface and knead vigorously. Roll out the dough to the thickness of a finger.

4. Spread the nut mixture over the dough, leaving a gap of about 1in (3cm) between the mixture and the dough edge. Roll up the dough. Using a long, sharp knife, cut the roll in half lengthwise, leaving a section of about 2in (5cm) uncut at the end. Weave the two pieces together to form a braid. Squeeze the cut ends of the braid together.

5. Place the braid on the baking tray. Bake it in the middle of the oven for about 45 minutes until it is golden-brown. Remove it from the oven and let cool.

6. Mix together the rum and confectioner's sugar to make a glaze. Brush the glaze over the braid. Let it dry for about 15 minutes before cutting it into inch-thick slices.

MAKES 1 YEAST BRAID (ABOUT 15 SLICES)
Preparation time:
 45 minutes
Rising time:
 1 hour 15 minutes

1 recipe yeast dough
 (see p. 137)
flour, for the work surface
4 tbsp raisins
7oz (200g) heavy cream
7oz (200g) ground
 hazelnuts
4 tbsp bread crumbs
5½oz (150g) sugar
1 package vanilla sugar or
 1 tsp pure vanilla extract
½ tsp ground cinnamon

FOR THE GLAZE
2 tbsp rum
5½oz (150g) confectioner's
 sugar

Berry cake with sour cream

By now, everyone is full. But this cake, with its many different kinds of fresh summer berries and its creamy filling, is irresistible! It is also a fabulous cake to take along with you to a biergarten or on a picnic.

SERVES 12
Preparation time:
    40 minutes
Baking time: 45 minutes

FOR THE CAKE
7oz (200g) all-purpose flour
½ package double-acting
    baking powder
4½oz (125g) unsalted
    butter, softened
4½oz (125g) sugar
1 package vanilla sugar or
    1 tsp pure vanilla extract
2 large eggs
3½fl oz (100ml) whole milk

FOR THE TOPPING
3 eggs
1¾oz (50g) sugar
14oz (400g) sour cream
2.2lb (1kg) mixed berries
    (such as blackberries,
    blueberries, raspberries,
    and red currants)

YOU WILL ALSO NEED
11-in (28-cm) springform
    pan
oil, for the pan
bread crumbs, for the pan

1. Preheat the oven to 350°F (180°C). Brush the inside of the springform pan with oil. Sprinkle the pan sparsely with bread crumbs.

2. To make the cake batter, mix the flour and baking powder together. In a bowl, cream together the butter, sugar, and vanilla sugar or vanilla extract. Beat in the eggs one at a time. Add the flour mixture and the milk, and mix together to make a smooth batter. Pour the batter into the springform pan and smooth the top. Bake in the middle of the oven for about 15 minutes.

3. To make the topping, beat the eggs and sugar until light and creamy. Add the sour cream, and beat again until thick and creamy.

4. Remove the cake from the oven and top it with the berries. Pour the cream mixture over the cake and bake it in the middle of the oven for 30 minutes until done.

TIP: To make a baking tray full of cake about 16×12×1in (40×30×2.5cm) in size, simply double the ingredients. If berries are not in season, you still can make the cake using mixed frozen berries.

Cherry pudding

1. Preheat the oven to 350°F (180°C). Generously butter 6 ovenproof glass dishes that each hold 1 cup (250ml). Cut the bread into small cubes. Place them in a bowl. Stem and pit the cherries and add them to the bread.

2. Separate the eggs. Beat the egg whites until they form stiff peaks. Whisk together the egg yolks, milk, sugar, and cinnamon. Pour the egg mixture over the bread cubes. Mix everything together well. Fold into the egg whites.

3. Pour the pudding mixture into the dishes and dot each with small flecks of butter. Bake the puddings in the middle of the oven for about 30 minutes. Serve warm or cold right out of the dishes.

MAKES 6 PUDDINGS
Preparation time:
   35 minutes
Baking time: 30 minutes

10½oz (300g) country-style
   bread, several days old
10½oz (300g) cherries
2 large eggs
7fl oz (200ml) whole milk
2 tbsp sugar
½ tsp ground cinnamon
2 tbsp butter, plus more for
   the dishes

Blueberry cheesecakes

1. Preheat the oven to 350°F (180°C). Brush 6 ovenproof glass dishes, each holding 1 cup (250ml), with oil. Combine the semolina, baking powder, and vanilla pudding.

2. Cream together the butter and sugar in a bowl. Beat in the eggs one by one. Add the quark or yogurt, lemon juice, and the semolina mixture, and beat until thick and creamy.

3. Fold in the blueberries. Fill the ovenproof dishes with the cheesecake mixture and bake them in the middle of the oven for about 30 minutes. Remove from the oven and serve warm or cold right out of the dishes.

MAKES 6 PUDDINGS
Preparation time:
   35 minutes
Baking time: 30 minutes

4½oz (125g) semolina
1 tsp baking powder
1 package vanilla pudding
   mix (not instant)
9oz (250g) unsalted butter
9oz (250g) sugar
4 eggs
2.2lb (1kg) quark (or a thick,
   plain, non-fat yogurt)
juice of 1 lemon
7oz (200g) blueberries

Chocolate almond cookies

These cookies make a great snack and taste good with a coffee in a biergarten. And the chunks of chocolate won't stick to your fingers!

MAKES ABOUT 20 COOKIES
Preparation time:
  30 minutes
Baking time: 10 minutes

3½oz (100g) blanched
  almonds
1¾oz (50g) dark chocolate
2½oz (75g) dried apricots
4½oz (125g) unsalted
  butter, softened
3½oz (100g) brown sugar
1 package vanilla sugar or
  1 tsp pure vanilla extract
2 large eggs
7oz (200g) light spelt flour
1 tbsp cocoa powder
4 tbsp whole milk

1. Preheat the oven to 350°F (180°C). Line a baking tray with parchment paper. Coarsely chop the almonds and the chocolate. Finely chop the apricots.

2. Cream together the butter, sugar, and vanilla sugar or vanilla extract in a bowl. Beat in the eggs one at a time. Add the flour, cocoa powder, almonds, chocolate, apricots, and milk, and combine to make a smooth dough.

3. Drop heaped tablespoons of dough about ½in (1cm) thick and 2in (5cm) in diameter onto the baking tray. Bake the cookies in the middle of the oven for about 10 minutes.

4. Lift the parchment paper, with the baked cookies on it, off the baking tray. Place it on a large wire rack to cool completely. Store the cookies in an airtight container.

TIP: These cookies can be varied as desired. Depending on what you have on hand, you can use hazelnuts, walnuts, cashews, candied ginger, white chocolate, or other dried fruits, instead of almonds, chocolate, and apricots. To give the cookies a bit more crunch, you can also use regular spelt flour instead of light spelt flour.

Fruit popsicles

A biergarten visit means fun for the whole family. While the adults are enjoying a drink and some food, there's nothing better to give the little ones than a popsicle—or perhaps even two!

1. To make the lemon popsicles, bring the lemon peel, sugar, and 1 cup of water to a boil in a small pot. Let cool and remove the lemon peel.

2. Stir the lemon juice into the syrup. Fill the mixture into 10 popsicle molds, insert the sticks, and leave the molds in the freezer for at least 4 hours.

3. To make the strawberry popsicles, purée the strawberries with the sugar, elderflower syrup, and lemon juice. Fill the mixture into 10 popsicle molds, insert the sticks, and leave the molds in the freezer for at least 4 hours.

4. To make the lime popsicles, mix the apple juice together with the lime syrup and lemon juice. Fill the mixture into 10 popsicle molds, insert the sticks, and leave the molds in the freezer for at least 4 hours.

5. To remove the popsicles from the molds, hold them briefly under running warm water until they loosen.

TIP: Popsicles come in countless flavors. This is because you can use every type of puréed fruit, fruit syrup, and fruit juice to fill into popsicle molds and freeze. Just try out any flavor you like.

MAKES 10 OF EACH FLAVOR
Preparation time:
    30 minutes
Freezing time: 4 hours

FOR THE LEMON POPSICLES
peel from an organic lemon
    (about 1in/3cm long)
1 cup sugar
freshly squeezed juice
    of 4 lemons

FOR THE STRAWBERRY POPSICLES
1lb 2oz (500g) strawberries
1 tbsp confectioner's sugar
4 tbsp elderflower syrup
freshly squeezed juice
    of 1 lemon

FOR THE APPLE LIME POPSICLES
1¾ cups (400ml) unfiltered
    apple juice
¼ cup lime syrup
freshly squeezed juice
    of 1 lemon

YOU WILL ALSO NEED
10 popsicle molds
    with sticks

Summery fruit salad

This combination of sweet, sour, and tangy fruits and berries tastes wonderful and makes a perfect summer dessert. If you like, you can top the fruit salad with a scoop of vanilla ice cream.

SERVES 4

Preparation time:
25 minutes

9oz (250g) mixed stone fruits (such as apricots, mirabelles, plums)
9oz (250g) mixed berries (strawberries, raspberries, red currants, and black currants)
3 tbsp brown sugar
4 tbsp cherry schnapps (kirschwasser)
freshly squeezed juice of 1 lemon
zest of ½ an organic lemon

1. Halve and pit the stone fruits. Depending on their size, cut the apricots and plums into quarters or eighths lengthwise. Place the cut fruit in a large bowl.

2. Hull the strawberries and, depending on their size, cut them into halves or quarters. Add the strawberries, raspberries, red currants, and black currants to the mixed stone fruit.

3. Stir together the sugar, cherry schnapps, lemon juice, and lemon zest, and dribble it over the fruit. Carefully toss the fruit salad and serve.

TIP: This salad can be prepared ahead of time. It is ideal to take along to the biergarten or on a picnic. To prevent the fruit from becoming too mushy, keep the sugar and schnapps mixture separate in a jar. Just before serving, dribble it over the salad and toss gently.

If certain fruits listed here aren't readily available, you can substitute any kind of fruits you like. Mirabelles, red currants, and black currants, for instance, are traditional, but may be difficult to find.

Beer shandies

In a biergarten, people usually drink beer and "Radler" or "Russn," which are shandies based on Hell and Weissbier, respectively, in giant liter glasses. At home, the glasses can be smaller and the mixes fruitier. These two shandies are quickly mixed and very refreshing.

1. To make the elderflower shandy, pour the sparkling mineral water into two glasses. Add elderflower syrup to taste and stir. Add the beer and serve immediately.

2. To make the grapefruit shandy, pour the grapefruit soda into two glasses. Add the Weissbier, making sure to also add the yeast that has settled at the bottom of the bottle. Cut the slice of grapefruit in half, place one half in each glass, and serve immediately.

VARIATION: To make a classic "Radler" shandy, mix 2 cups of clear, sparkling lemonade with 2 cups of Hell beer. To make a classic "Russn" shandy, mix 2 cups of clear, sparkling lemonade with 2 cups of Weissbier.

MAKES 4 CUPS OF EACH KIND OF DRINK
Preparation time:
    5 minutes for each kind

FOR THE ELDERFLOWER SHANDY
2 cups sparkling mineral
    water
elderflower syrup
2 cups Hell or
    alcohol-free beer

FOR THE GRAPEFRUIT SHANDY
2 cups grapefruit-flavored
    soda
2 cups Weissbier or
    alcohol-free Weissbier
1 slice of grapefruit

Bavarian German for the biergarten

If you want to understand your neighbors in the biergarten, here is a little guide to the Bavarian dialect to help you out. If you don't want to be outed immediately as a "Zuagroaster," a stranger, you'll need a lot of practice before you can order a "Brezn" and a "Mass" without an accent.

A

aufbrezln to make oneself chic

Auszog'ne a fried, flat donut with a high, soft edge that is thin and crisp inside

B

Bam tree

Biafuizl beer coaster, often with a brewery logo on it

Brezn soft pretzels. A favorite Bavarian baked good, gnawed on with gusto by countless toothless babies.

Butterbrezn soft pretzels sliced in half horizontally and spread with a thick layer of butter. A beloved snack.

Brotzeit traditionally a snack enjoyed by farmers, alpine shepherds, tradespeople, students, and hikers. It is perfect for taking along to the biergarten. It can consist of bread, various kinds of cheese and sausage, meat in aspic, ham, Obatzda, radishes, and daikon radish, for example.

bschdäin order food and beer

D

Deandl young girl

Dotschn plump, rather inflexible woman

F

fesch chic

fei an untranslatable fill word, which doesn't stop the Bavarians from using it in almost every sentence

Föhn a warm, dry wind that comes from the Alps. It is considered responsible for everything, such as giving people headaches and making them feel very tired.

G

Gell/geh? Eh? Isn't it true?

Grantler a person who is in a bad mood

greißlig horrible

griabig super

Griaß Di/Grüß Gott good day

Gseichts cured (meat)

gsund healthy

H

Haxn pork hock or hocks, not to be confused with "Haxen," which means legs. The crunchy skin calls for strong teeth.

Helles a bottom fermented, golden-yellow beer with a specific gravity of 11–13% and an alcohol content of 4.5–6% per volume

Hendl grilled chicken

Himmiherrgottsakramentzefix- halleluja long curse word

Hoibä half a liter of beer

Hoiz voa da Hüttn a well-endowed woman

J

ja mei a standard Bavarian expression meaning "it was always like this, it is like this, and it will always be like this."

K

Kaas cheese

Käinrin female waiter

Knödl dumplings made from potatoes or bread

Krachlederne traditional Bavarian leather shorts

L

laar empty, all drunken up, order a new one

Leberkässemmi bread roll filled with a slice of just-baked luncheon meat called "Leberkaese"

Löffi spoon

M

Mass 1 liter of beer

Mei fill word, usually in combination with "ja" (ja mei), meaning "so it is"

N

Noagal the dregs in a glass

O

Oachkatzl squirrel

obandln flirting

Obatzda or Obatzter or Obazda. A kind of soft cheese spread. Originally it was made from old, leftover cheese. The recipe is usually a secret. The ingredients are Camembert cheese, other soft cheeses, butter, paprika, and often caraway seeds and/or onions.

P

Pressack head cheese, a delicacy made from pork

Pfiad Di/Eana good-bye

R

Radla "Radler." A shandy made with light beer (Hell) and clear, sparkling lemonade

Radi radish

Radieserl red radishes—a healthy touch of color on every "Brotzeit" plate

ratschn to chat casually with one another

Russn or Russ. A shandy that is made with Weissbier and clear, sparkling lemonade

S

Saupreiß unpleasant person who comes from anywhere other than Bavaria

schbeim to vomit

Schmankerl tasty Bavarian product or dish

Semmi bread roll

Steckerlfisch am Stab gegrillter fish

T

Taxler taxi driver

U

umasonst free or, also, in vain

W

Watschn a slap

Wiaschdl sausage

Wuaschtsalad sausage salad

Weissbier wheat beer

X

xund see "gsund"

Xang song

Z

Zamperl a small dog and welcome guest in every biergarten. It always gets fresh water from the biergarten owner.

zuabrosdn the act of toasting one other

zuagroast anyone whose family tree does not have at least five generations of native Bavarians on it

zutzeln careful sucking out of the inside of a "Weisswurst," a traditional Bavarian veal sausage, usually served poached

zwengs because of

zwida in a bad mood

Zwoa Mass and oa Brezn! Two liters of Hell beer and a pretzel, please!

Biergarten tips

Picnic basket basics

Aside from the food, you'll need unbreakable plates, utensils, small cutting boards, a sharp knife for slicing, for example, the bread, tomatoes, and sausages, salt and pepper shakers, and a plastic bag for the dirty dishes.

And don't forget, we also eat with our eyes, which holds true for the biergarten, too. For a well-laid picnic table, bring a tablecloth (it doesn't have to be checked) and napkins. Tea lights help create a romantic mood when it gets dark.

Perfectly packed

So that the food arrives intact and nothing leaks, packing your picnic the right way is crucial. Pack salads into plastic containers with lids that seal tightly. Fill savory butter, spreads, and salad dressings into glass jars with twist-off lids. Springform pans give quiches and cakes support. Wrap the pans in generous amounts of plastic wrap, then wrap them tightly in aluminum foil.

Place hot food such as hamburger patties, baked potatoes, and roast pork in pre-warmed, deep casserole dishes. To retain the heat, wrap the dishes in plenty of aluminum foil and then in thick layers of newspaper. Place the hot dishes in an insulated bag. Place cold food in a cooler bag. It will stay cold and if you use enough frozen gel packs, even popsicles will remain frozen.

Last minute plans

After a dreary day, the sun suddenly peeks through the clouds and you quickly make arrangements to meet friends for a picnic. Of course, you want to bring along some food, even though there is no time to go shopping. Dishes such as Obatzda (page 17), savory butter spreads (page 30), potato and sour cream spread (page 25), sausage salad (page 33), cheese and pepper salad (page 38), and cherry pudding (page 145) are quickly made with ingredients you probably have in your refrigerator or pantry, such as fresh cheese, Brie cheese, Camembert cheese, deli sausage, red and green bell peppers, onions, cherries, and sour cream.

A biergarten party at home

Is it pouring outside? Do you really miss the biergarten atmosphere and that summer feeling? It's time to throw a biergarten party at home with family and friends! Serve grilled spare ribs, sausages and steak, homemade salads, spreads, dill pickles, soft pretzels, and, of course, something sweet. Rent some wooden picnic tables and benches. Decorate with Bavarian white-and-blue diamond-patterned tablecloths, napkins, garlands, and paper lanterns. Good food, a keg of beer or two (where available), a selection of bottled beers, and some non-alcoholic drinks will surely satisfy everyone.

Index

LIST OF GERMAN RECIPES

The Authors

Julia Skowronek is Bavarian by choice and lives in Munich. After her professional training as a chef, she pursued a career as a cookbook author and food stylist, focusing on refined everyday cuisine. Food photographer Brigitte Sporrer was born in Munich and still lives there. The beauty of Bavarian food and culinary culture are very dear to her. She has contributed images to several cookbooks.

Recipes Julia Skowronek, Munich
Feature texts Carolin Fried, Munich
Translation Barbara Hopkinson, Toronto
Photography Brigitte Sporrer. Exceptions: p. 2 center right (Paulaner), p. 2 below (Michael Nagy, Presseamt München), p. 4/5 (Stock Food/Strauss, F.), p. 6 (Stock Food/Schmid, Ulrike), p. 20 below (Paulaner), p. 53 (Paulaner), p. 119 (Paulaner), p. 53 center right (Manfi B.)
Editor Petra Teetz, Cadolzburg
Graphic Design, typography, illustrations Wilhelm Schäfer (Typocepta), Cologne
Repro Medienservice Farbsatz, Neuried/Munich

Publishing Manager Monika Schlitzer
Managing Editor Elke Homburg
Production Manager Dorothee Whittaker
Production Sophie Schiela
US Editors Jenny Siklos, Allison Singer
US Designer Jessica Lee
US Editorial Director Stephanie Farrow

First American edition, 2015
Published in the United States by DK Publishing
345 Hudson Street, New York, NY 10014

15 16 17 18 19 10 9 8 7 6 5 4 3 2 1
001—275124—Mar/15
Copyright © 2014 Dorling Kindersley Limited
A Penguin Random House Company
All rights reserved

Published in Germany by Dorling Kindersley Verlag GmbH, München, 2014

A catalog record for this book is available from the Library of Congress.
ISBN 978-1-4654-3401-2

Printed and bound in China

DK books are available at special discounts when purchased in bulk for sales promotions, premiums, fund-raising, or educational use. For details, contact: DK Publishing Special Markets, 345 Hudson Street, New York, NY 10014 or SpecialSales@dk.com.

www.dk.com